Leading Innovation and Change Management - Characteristics of Innovative Companies

How are the top five global innovative companies
sustaining their competitive advantage?

Osman M. Gunu

International

iLEAD ACADEMY

Leadership Education and Associate Development Academy

Osman M. Gunu, 2011. *Leading Innovation and Change Management-Characteristics of Innovative Companies.*

Produced by: ILEAD Academy, LLC

Cover design by: Cagri Tanyar
Technical coordinator: Bahaudin G. Mujtaba

ISBN 10:   1-936237-05-9
ISBN 13:   978-1-936237-05-0

1:   BUS065000   Business & Economics : Total Quality Management
2:   BUS087000   Business & Economics : Production & Operations Management
3:   BUS071000   Business & Economics : Leadership

ILEAD Academy, LLC
Davie, Florida. United States
www.ileadacademy.com

This book is dedicated to my father
who taught me what truthfulness
and humbleness can do for you in
life. May he rest in absolute peace.
Also to my beautiful daughters
and step daughter Zarah,
Hamida and Nora.

Table of Contents

Preface

Innovation has no handbook according to one of the most powerful CEOs in the global market place. There are several definitions of innovation out there in journals, textbooks, newsletters and what have you; however, there are key elements of innovation cannot be ignored in an attempt to define the term. In defining innovation, you must keep in mind cost effectiveness, efficiency and more importantly the ability to read customers' minds and anticipate their needs, wants, and desires. Being innovative doesn't end after anticipating customer needs and wants. Being innovative ends when an organization is able to research and design the anticipated needs and wants into products and services in a timely and cost effective manner. The top five most innovative multinational organizations according to Boston Consulting Group (BCG) study which is the core of this book have sustained their competitiveness in the ever changing global market place because those companies are able to read customers' minds, anticipate what they need to design programs to translate those needs into products and services in a timely and cost effective manner.

Apple, Google, Toyota, Microsoft, and Nintendo are the top five most innovative multinational organizations according to BCG. I've intentionally made this book concise because of my experience with adult learners as well as the traditional in-class student body. This book contains all the secrets and strategies that you need to restructure your company as a learning organization. How to become a learning organization and how to put what you've learned into practice is all that this book is about. What are these five top innovative multinational organizations doing different from other organizations? What are they focusing on? What is on the minds of these top CEOs? You will learn all the concepts in this easy to read five chapter book.

This is an easy to read book which examines the characteristics of the top five global innovative companies (Apple, Google, Toyota, Microsoft and Nintendo). Interviews with some of the CEOs demonstrate that they believe innovation has no manual. Developing a breakthrough product is a matter of chance. The book has examined the perspectives of the CEOs interviewed and how they are oiling their innovation engine to stay competitive in the ever changing global market.

The book is designed for business schools seeking to expose students to leadership and entrepreneurial skills of the 21st Century. Each chapter begins with case analyses of the company; examines the innovation policy of the company; the company's marketing strategy, human resource policy as well as the industry overview. The chapters discuss what each company is uniquely doing to sustain its competitive advantage in the ever changing global market. Each chapter examines the importance of developing creative and innovative workforce; and why continuous organizational learning is critical for survival.

Acknowledgements

So much of what I know about innovation and change management, organization theory and management I have learned from Dr. Anthony Petroy classes from Argosy University. We reviewed and commented on several case studies on successful and failed leaderships in multinational organizations. "Leading Innovation and Change Management - Characteristics of Innovative Companies" is designed for business schools seeking to expose students to leadership and entrepreneurial skills of the 21st Century. This book would not have been possible without Dr. Petroy's classes.

First, nothing is possible without the blessings of the Almighty God; the Creator of the Heavens and the Earth. The most Merciful and Forgiving God; thank you for everything you have done and continue to do in my life.

Second, my warmest thanks go to my loving wife Freda for entertaining my midnight "candles." To my family and to all my colleagues who have reviewed and critiqued the book there is no enough space to mention your names you know yourselves. Thank you for your time and comments. If you have additional comments you can contact me at osmanmasahudu@yahoo.com.

Third, I would like to acknowledge my mentors at the Washington Office, United States Department of Agriculture (USDA)-Forest Service, Financial Management Group – Karren Alexander, Rico Clarke, LaVeta Charity, and Gail McCrary. I appreciate your mentorship.

Finally, special thanks go to Dr. Bahaudin G. Mujtaba, Associate Professor of Management at the H. Wayne Huizenga School of Business and Entrepreneurship of Nova Southeastern University for his assistance and support in publishing the book.

Osman M. Gunu

1 – Why Apple is Considered Number One Most Innovative Company

I nnovation is important for success in today's turbulent and competitive workplace. "Innovation management is a critical discipline for both academics and practitioners. The capacity of organizations to innovate is determined by multiple factors that relate both to their own internal organization and to their market environment and the task of generating and then converting ideas into usable and marketable products requires high levels of inter-functional co-ordination and integration."[1]

Chapter Learning Objectives

- Understanding strategies Apple uses to stay as number one most innovative company in the personal computers and mobile communication industry.
- Comprehending Apple's marketing and innovative strategies.
- Gaining elementary comprehension of value innovation as well as blue and red ocean strategies.
- Exploring the innovation journey as well as the sources of innovative ideas.
- Recognizing the importance of customer-driven innovation.
- Examining challenges organizations face in building sustainable innovation programs/innovation inhibitors.
- Understanding various interventions to innovation inhibitors.
- Recognizing Apple's Strengths, Weaknesses, Opportunities, and Threats in the global market place.

Introduction

The global economic tsunami has caused many multinational organizations to shrink their Research and Development budgets, consolidate subsidiaries and functional areas across entities. Consolidating functional areas across entities in the global marketplace has caused many multinational organizations to lack behind in innovation and change management because employees are over-tasked and stressed. Sustained competitive advantage is largely based on the ability of organizations to effectively manage their skilled employees as well as their innovation processes. What is Apple doing different from other multinational organizations that has allowed it to sustain its competitive advantage? Apple Corporation has demonstrated the importance of talent management and motivation within their organization. Effective talent management and motivation has enabled Apple to consistently maintain its number one position for two fiscal years as a global most innovative company. For fiscal years 2008 and 2009 respectively, Apple has kept its number one spot as the most innovative company in the global marketplace[2]. This chapter and the subsequent chapters will be developed based on the top five most innovative multinational corporations in the global marketplace. What are the top five multinational corporations doing different from the rest of the global companies? What are the fundamental characteristics of these companies? What are the leadership styles as well as the organizational culture, mission and vision of these companies? These questions and more will be addressed in the detailed chapters of this book. This book is a five chapter book based on the characteristics and innovation strategies of the top five most innovative organizations in the global marketplace.

The methodology for selecting the top five most innovative multinational corporations is primarily based on Boston Consulting Group (BCG) survey. Annually, BCG sends its carefully selected 20 questions poll to senior executives of multinational corporations in the global marketplace; an average of 2,700 participants respond anonymously to those questions. In those questions, participants were asked to name multinational corporations that consistently offer inventive products, customer experiences, business models, or processes. One interesting part of the poll is that, participants who selected or chose their own corporations are automatically disqualified[3]. BCG will factor in the financial performance of the organizations that have higher votes and the final list is analyzed based on stock returns, revenue growth, margin growth as well as participants' perception of each organization based on product innovativeness, customer experience, process efficiency, and business model.

Apple and Google corporations appear to be the most dominant innovative corporations in the global marketplace for some time now. I will explore what each of these corporations is doing differently in detailed case study for the rest of the chapter. Chapter one will discuss Apple and its innovative strategies; what Apple is doing differently from other multinational corporations.

Apple Corporation Case Study – What Apple is Doing Different

Apple Inc. is a multinational software and technology corporation headquartered in Cupertino, California. Founded in April 1976 by three like minded entrepreneurs: Steve Jobs, Steve Wozniak, and Ronald Wayne. Apple has about 34,300 employees worldwide. Apple's core competency is spread through multiple business areas but predominantly in personal computers, mobile communication devices as well as networking solutions. As of 2009, Apple reported total assets of $47.5 billion, revenues of $42.9 billion, operating income of $11.7 billion as well as total equity of $31.6 billion[4]. Apple's success is based on creating innovative high quality products and services, as well as demonstrating integrity in every business interaction. Apple's principles of business conduct define the way they do business worldwide. The organization's principles of business conduct include: honesty, respect, confidentiality, community, and compliance.

Honesty: Apple demonstrates honesty and high ethical standards in all their business transactions.

Respect: Apple treats their customers, suppliers, employees, and others with respect and courtesy.

Confidentiality: Apple protects the confidentiality of its information as well as the information of their customers, suppliers, and employees.

Community: Apple conducts business in a manner that benefits the communities in which they operate or transact business.

Compliance: Apple ensures their business decisions comply with all applicable laws and regulations.

Apple delivers a stream of extremely well-designed products that create and build new markets from existing technologies and platforms; has the ability to create demand by understanding customers' needs and anticipating new ones, reintroduces new products at the right time and effectively markets them. Apple has built a culture that encourages innovation and accepts all risks that come with it[5].

Every product and service Apple provides is for their customers because the organization focuses so much on providing innovative, high quality products and services for its existing and potential customers. It is evident from the words of the Chief Executive Officer that there is no handbook or manual for innovation. Innovation has no handbook or manual. You have to capitalize on it even if it's a by-product or an afterthought. So the iPhone, arguably the most significant technological device of the 21st Century, was actually an afterthought that came into being while Apple was drawing up plans for the iPad[6]. In an interview, Steve Jobs couldn't keep a secret; he openly shared how the revolutionary iPhone came to being. "I'll tell you a secret, the iPhone began with a tablet, my God, I said this would make a great phone; so we shelved the tablet and built the iPhone" – Steve Jobs, Apple CEO. Steve Jobs attributes Apple's innovativeness to its open culture and organizational structure where the customer is always the focus. "I have one of the best jobs in the world. I get to hang out with some of the most talented, committed people around, and together we get to play in this sandbox and build these cool products. Apple is an incredibly collaborative company. You know how many committees we have at Apple? Zero. We're structured like a start-up. We're the biggest start-up on the planet. And we all meet once a week to discuss our business" – Steve Jobs.

Apple markets its products and services globally through its online stores, retail stores, direct sales, third party wholesalers, resellers as well as value added resellers. The organization markets a variety of third party Mac, iPhone, and iPod compatible products and services including application software, printers, storage devices, speakers, headphones, and a variety of other accessories and peripherals through its online and retail stores. Apple products and services are marketed to consumers, small and mid-sized businesses, education, enterprise, government, and other consumers. As of 2009, apple had 273 retail stores, including 217 stores in the United States and 56 stores globally[7]. Though most firms go to great lengths to disrupt innovation and entrepreneurship, few are really good at these activities.

Apple Innovation and Marketing Strategy

High investment in Research and Development (R&D), and holistic strategy in the consumer market in a form of direct sale as well as the use of consultants at the point of sale are helping the organization to re-invent marketing and innovation. Apple has great leadership that is able to pick the brains of the talented employees and put the ideas into good use. The following is an extract from an interview where Steve Jobs was asked how he manages for innovation within Apple; and also emphasizes the importance of having talented and committed employees who have the passion for excellence. He emphasizes firmness and prioritization:

> We hire people who want to make the best things in the world. You'd be surprised how hard people work around here. They work nights and weekends, sometimes not seeing their families for a while. Sometimes people work through Christmas to make sure the tooling is just right at some factory in some corner of the world so our product comes out the best it can be. People care so much, and it shows. I get asked a lot why Apple's customers are so loyal. It's not because they belong to the Church of Mac! That's ridiculous. It's because when you buy our products, and three months later you get stuck on something, you quickly figure out how to get past it. And you think, "Wow, someone over there at Apple actually thought of this" And then three months later you try to do something you hadn't tried before and it works, and you think "Hey, they thought of that, too." And then six months later it happens again. There's almost no product in the world that you have that experience with, but you have it with a Mac. And you have it with an iPod.
>
> Within Apple, innovation comes from people meeting up in the hallways or calling each other at 10:30 at night with a new idea, or because they realized something that shoots holes in how we've been thinking about a problem. It's ad hoc meetings of six people called by someone who thinks he has figured out the coolest new thing ever and who wants to know what other people think of his idea.

And it comes from saying no to 1,000 things to make sure we don't get on the wrong track or try to do too much. We're always thinking about new markets we could enter, but it's only by saying no that you can concentrate on the things that are really important. Within Apply we go back and forth a lot as we work on our projects. And we've got such great people in the top executive team that I've been able to move about half of the day-to-day management of the company to them, so I can spend half my time on the new stuff, like the retail effort. I spent and continue to spend a lot of time on that. And I meet weekly for two or three hours with my OS X team. And there's the group doing our iLife applications. I get to spend my time on the forward-looking stuff. My top executives take half the other work off my plate. They love it, and I love it. When I got back here, Apple had forgotten who we were. Remember that "Think Different" ad campaign we ran featuring great innovators from Einstein to Muhammad Ali to Gandhi. It was certainly for customers to some degree, but it was even more for Apple itself.

You can tell a lot about a person by who his or her heroes are. That ad was to remind us of whom our heroes are and who we are. We forgot that for a while. Companies sometimes forget who they are. Sometimes they remember again, and sometimes they don't. Fortunately, we woke up. And we're on a really good track. We may not be the richest guy in the graveyard at the end of the day, but we're the best at what we do. And Apple is doing the best work in its history. I really believe that. And there's a lot more coming.

The CEO appears to be a results-oriented leader with lots of patience and passion; because vision inspires passion. Results-oriented leaders must have both a mission and a vision. Results mean little without purpose: a mission instills both the passion and the patience for the long journey. While vision inspires passion, many failed ventures are characterized by passion without patience[8].

Apple's Competitive Strategy

Apple believes continual investment in R&D is critical to the development and enhancement of innovative products and technologies. In addition, Apple continues to build and host a robust platform for the discovery and delivery of third party digital content and applications through the iTunes Store. Recently, Apple launched the APP Store that allows users to browse, search for, and purchase third party applications through either a Mac or Windows based computer or by wirelessly downloading directly to an iPhone or iPod touch. While Apple is widely recognized as a leading innovator in the personal computer, mobile communications and consumer electronics markets; Apple is also recognized as a leader in the emerging markets for distribution of digital content and applications. These markets are believed to be highly competitive and subject to aggressive pricing. To remain competitive in the global marketplace, Apple believes that increased investment in employee training and development, R&D, marketing, and aggressive advertising are necessary to maintain or expand its position in the markets it competes[9].

R&D Spending: Apple's R&D spending is focused on further developing its existing Mac line of personal computers, its operating system, application software, iPhone and iPods; developing new digital lifestyle, consumer and professional software application, as well as investment in new product areas and technologies. Apple believes increased investment in marketing and advertising programs are critical to increasing product and brand awareness[10]. R&D expenditures increased 20% or $224 million to $1.3 billion in 2009 compared to 2008[11]. These increases were due to increase in headcount in the current year to support expanded R&D activities and higher stock based compensation expenses. Apple's advertising costs are expensed as incurred. Advertising expense was $501 million, $486 million and $467 million for 2009, 2008, and 2007 respectively.

Distribution Channel: Apple utilizes a variety of direct and indirect distribution channels. Apple believes that sales of its innovative and differentiated products are enhanced by knowledgeable salespeople who can carry the value of the hardware, software, and peripheral integration, demonstrate the unique digital lifestyle solutions that are available on Mac computers as well as demonstrate the compatibility of the Mac with the Windows platform and networks. Apple believes further that providing a high quality sale and after sales support experience is critical to attracting new and retaining existing customers[12].

Revenue Recognition: Net sales consist primarily of revenue from the sales of hardware, software, digital content and applications, peripherals, service and support contracts. Apple recognizes revenue when persuasive evidence of an arrangement exists and delivery has occurred; the sales price is fixed or determinable, and collection is probable. Product is considered delivered to the customer once it has been shipped and title and risk of loss have been transferred. For most of Apple's product sales, these criteria are met at the time the product is shipped. For online sales to individuals, education customers in the U.S as well as certain other sales, Apple defers recognition of revenue until the customer receives the product because Apple retains a portion of the risk of loss on those sales during transit. In addition, Apple recognizes revenue from the sale of hardware products such as Mac computers, iPhones, iPods, and peripherals, software bundled with hardware that is essential to the functionality of the hardware, as well as third party digital content sold on the iTunes Store in accordance with general revenue recognition accounting principles[13].

According to W. Chan Kim and Renee Mauborgne in their best selling strategy and business book "*Blue Ocean Strategy – How to Create Uncontested Market Space and Make the Competition Irrelevant.*" They emphasize the importance of making your competition irrelevant and desist from competing with your rivals. Apple has desisted from competing with its rivals. Apple is making its rivals irrelevant in the overcrowded industry of personal computing and mobile communication. Kim and Mauborgne maintain that today's corporations like Apple and Google will succeed not by battling competition, but by creating "blue oceans" of uncontested market space ripe for growth. Creating uncontested market space ripe for growth means they will be creating what is termed as "value innovation."

Value Innovation

Value innovation occurs only when companies align innovation with utility, price, and cost positions.[14] A company is considered a valued innovation company when the company's innovative strategies are focused on projecting future needs of customers and designing appropriate strategies to meet and exceed those needs. With value innovation, companies focus on customers instead of on competition.

Every product and service Apple provides is for their customers because the organization focuses so much on providing innovative, high quality products and services for its existing and potential customers. In addition, Apple has created an environment where employees can communicate directly to their superiors with any innovative ideas regardless of the time of the day. Apple's leadership and employees have demonstrated trust and commitment by relying on each other to execute their innovative ideas on a daily basis. The innovative ideas are often customer centered.

Blue Ocean Strategy vs. Competition Based Strategy/Red Ocean Strategy:

Blue ocean strategy is designed to create new segments of customer demand by re-structuring traditional marketing strategies, focusing primarily on customers' present and future needs.[15] Competition Based Strategy or the Red Ocean Strategy exploits existing customer demand by ignoring future demands.

It is evident that Apple's success emanates from the utilization of the Blue Ocean Strategy. When Apple makes a product, Apple works to create uncontested market space by designing systems in place to anticipate and resolve future needs or challenges of the customer. Before a customer makes a complaint about Apple's product, a system has already been designed to anticipate and resolve the complaint. Therefore, the customer doesn't have to wait endlessly for solution. The solution has already been built into a sub-system.

Apple works diligently to make its competition irrelevant by heavily investing in its employee development as well as R&D. Empowering your employees to innovate and create products and services that cannot be duplicated by competition will make the competition irrelevant and helpless. When employees in a company are empowered to think freely and to react to customers' needs in a timely manner, eventually it translates into a sustained competitive advantage. Many multinational corporations continue to struggle with the challenge of how to raise their innovation games for the new competitive landscape, and most have long since reached the limits of trying to drive further growth through incremental refinements[16]. Apple has re-explored and captured the knowledge funnel by consistently innovating new ideas to win the global markets by staying on top of its existing and potential customers.

Whereas companies in the Red Ocean Strategy work to make the value-cost trade-off, companies like Apple have worked diligently to break the value-cost trade-off. Breaking the value-cost trade-off in a saturated or overcrowded industry like the mobile communication and personal computing industries sets the tone for sustained competitive advantage. Costs and quality are important elements especially in the personal computing and mobile communication industries; Apple understands this and has put a system in place to produce high quality products and services at affordable rates. By pinpointing and solving the mystery before the competition, Apple has created an initial efficiency advantage, by converting discovery of solution into algorithm. In addition, Apple has raised the efficiency advantage, lowered prices but not ignoring quality and dramatically enhanced the value position.[17]

The gestation period of an invention may last for many years, after which seemingly coincidental events occur that set the stage for innovation to be initiated.[18] It is no surprise that the invention of the revolutionary iPhone was an accident. Apple stumbled on the revolutionary iPhone during its innovative and creative strategies. Therefore, Apple's iPhone may be considered a by-product which has been re-designed to become the cash cow of the company. Great innovative ideas sometimes do not get to the commercial stage due to lack of focus, ambiguity, lack of patience, skilled personnel to advance the idea, and most importantly, lack of funding and good leadership.

Apple's leadership has demonstrated a great sense of passion and commitment to their innovative ideas from employees. Apple's leadership has been able to nurture innovative ideas, provide the required resources as well as the leadership needed to quickly move innovative ideas to commercialization. Apple's tremendous success in the personal computer, mobile communication devices and networking industry has also been attributed to senior management initiative to quickly develop leaders within their organization. Developing leaders within an organization must start right from day one.

The right strategy is to place equal emphasis on creating breakthroughs in buyer value and controlling costs. To be profitable in today's global competitive marketplace, organizations need to shift their attention and efforts from the competition to buyers; and more importantly by exploring existing demand in order to create new demand.[19] Apple has been instrumental in creating new demand and breakthroughs within the last seven years. R&D expenditures increased

20% or $224 million to $1.3 billion in 2009 compared to 2008. As of 2009, Apple had 273 retail stores, including 217 stores in the United States and 56 stores globally.

Sources of Innovation/Ideas

Where do companies get their innovative ideas? It is interesting to view the study conducted by IBM in 2006. IBM survey was based on in-person interviews of CEOs, general managers, senior public and business leaders around the world. As part of their research, IBM sought to unravel business model innovation – the new route to competitive advantage. When the CEOs were asked about the most important sources of ideas and innovation, the CEOs ranked employees as the most important source of innovative ideas. Employees were followed by external sources such as business partners and customers. You might be wondering what the ranking of internal R&D departments was. Surprisingly, internal R&D departments were ranked eighth in importance.[20] Research indicates that most of the major multinational organizations get their innovative ideas through outsourcing.[21] It is envisioned that in today's global competitive market environment, business partners can provide a source of innovative transformation by outsourcing the innovation to business partners who have the know-how and resources to develop the innovation to commercialization. Apple has been instrumental in developing its innovative ideas in-house while seeking expert advice if necessary. The question now becomes, how do organizations manage outsourcing of innovation to business partners effectively while maintaining their strategic competitiveness.[22] This section will discuss the three fundamental models of innovation outsourcing developed by Balor, Jha, and Awazu (2008). If properly executed, outsourcing to business partners can tremendously help organizations to achieve sustained competitive advantage; especially among organizations that don't have systems in place to handle and manage the innovation journey.

1. Outsourcing of Innovation Through External Knowledge Acquisition: According to Balor et al. (2008) outsourcing innovation through external acquisition has several benefits. First, they maintain that organizations can choose to purchase the best of breed and incur neither the cost nor the risk of in house innovation. Balor et al. (2008) add that in an era of specialized business, many organizations focus upon specific

areas of expertise, and their employees may not have the diversity and breadth of knowledge to develop technological or product innovations outside the organization's domain field or business model. The second benefit of innovation acquisition through external partners is that the acquiring organization can act in a nimble manner and acquire knowledge that arises out of developing needs. The researchers maintain further that when a need is recognized within an organization, the organization can search for and purchase the knowledge that will answer its need immediately. The innovation acquisition might take the form of a new technology, manufacturing procedures, or a product component. In those instances, an organization sidesteps the costly and sometimes lengthy R&D cycle and is able to seize solutions found to match core competencies and supplement organizational strengths. As the competitive environment is highly dynamic, being able to satisfy developing needs is critical.[23] The third benefit of outsourcing innovation through external knowledge acquisition is that, sometimes intellectual property protects particular pieces of knowledge. When that occurs, an organization may be able to work collaboratively with a business partner who has the rights to a particular patent in order to use a specific product component or piece of technology.

2. Outsourcing Innovation Through Strategic Alliances: Balor et al. (2008), maintain that one of the main motivations for the creation of innovation focused alliances is to source new knowledge and learning. For instance, when two organizations are already competitively strong, one or both parties may want to acquire critical knowledge, while maintaining their capabilities.[24] Strategic alliances enable organizations to capture the technology of their competitor or other organization and more importantly may help close skill gaps faster than internal development would permit. Strategic alliances foster intense interactions according to Balor et al. (2008) and that the collaboration enables the transfer of tacit knowledge between members.

3. Outsourcing Innovation Through Open Source Model: The open source movement originated from the software development field, however, can be applied to any area where knowledge becomes publicly available. With open source

model of innovation outsourcing, open source developing companies utilize their own resources to develop innovative products or services which are afterwards made publicly available for adoption and adaptation by end users or competitors. One interesting aspect of open source model is that organizations or individuals involved in open source modeling do not expect any return on their investment and most importantly, do not care about free riding. The questions that may be asked are, why would an organization choose to engage in open source type innovation? Or what drives an organization to allocate resources to developing products they then provide for free to users?[25] The answer is that, open source organizations or individuals gain substantially increased innovation capabilities and can derive financial benefits from drawing upon and contributing to commonly held goods, services, and knowledge.[26]

Customer-Driven Innovation

Organizations in today's competitive marketplace are increasingly recognizing the need to innovate in partnership with their customers. They are changing their innovation strategies from innovating for customers to innovating with customers and involving those customers in a process of knowledge co-creation. Customer innovation has become an essential strategy for organizational survival.[27] Apple's market success is much attributed to the company's ability to co-create products and services. Co-creating products and services means organizations must allow customers to drive their innovation engine. According to Fogg, Husson, Mulligan & Wiramihardja (2010) every new product that Apple launches, Apple secures enormous attention, in part due to Apple's cultivated magnetism in anticipating customer needs. Forrester, a technology and market research company that provides pragmatic advice to global leaders in business and technology, advises that organizations must see through the magic by using threat analysis to predict what competitors and peers will do next by evaluating their capabilities and intent together. Fogg et al. (2010) add that when Apple launches products, such as the iPad, into a new market, every competitor rightly re-evaluates its product strategy. But there's more substance than magic to Apple's success than either its fans or its critics' credit. For competitors, this is reassuring: It's easier to replicate substance than magic. Companies must now offer software and hardware that's compatible with Apple products and services in order to survive. Apple's "let the customer drive strategy" has made competition difficult to catch up. Therefore, Apple's competition must compete using Apple's products to succeed in numerous markets due to the rising significance of Apple's customer base and their inclusiveness in designing the products and services. Product managers must learn from Apple and closely tie longer-term strategy to immediate tactics. They must ensure that their products always deliver a high-quality and convenient set of benefits, regardless of price point. If not, they must take the hard decision to delay launch until such time that they do.[28] Delaying product launch means inability to quickly collect customers' ideas and commercialize them in a timely manner. Organizations must both collect and develop ideas from customers quickly; they also have to commercialize the ideas rapidly.[29] Rapid commercialization of products and services is one of the core competencies of Apple.

Identifying the Customer:

Customer driven innovation companies have been utilizing their lead product users who they believe possess the knowledge they need to better help in the design and development of new products and services. The lead product users can also help the organizations improve their existing products and services. The ideas that most of these companies gather from their lead product users is unparalleled. For instance, in 2007 some organizations were not interested in Apple's iPhone and iPad due to information security concerns. Apple was able to address this issue through customer workshops coupled with innovative strategies to make the iPhone and iPad the most secured communication device customers have ever used on the market. Keeping corporate information secured is one of the major challenges of most multinational corporations including federal, state and local governments.

Analyzing Customer Information:

How do organizations analyze customer information? Most multinational organizations, medium and small size companies utilize their point-of sale systems to gather and process customer behaviors related to the products and services they purchase. Analysis of customer information helps organizations customize their products and services to suit the needs of their customers. Effective analysis of customer information may also help organizations improve the marketing of their existing products and services. For example, Apple's websites, online services, interactive applications, email messages, and advertisements utilize "cookies" and other technologies such as pixel tags and web beacons to analyze and understand customer behaviors. These sophisticated technologies help Apple better understand user behaviors. Apple also gathers information about which websites users have visited and what they were looking for. These technologies are primarily used to target customers with certain products and services. Apple takes customers' private information seriously.

Information security is critical for the federal government as well. The two landmark information security legislations that the federal government passed in recent years include the Federal Information Security Management Act (FISMA) of 2008 and the old Privacy Act of 1974. These Acts provide the framework for securing federal government information including Personally Identifiable Information (PII) of federal contractors and employees. As part of these Acts, federal agencies and departments are required to annually report to the Office of Management and Budget (OMB) and Congress the effectiveness of their privacy and information security programs.

Business Process-Customer Interactions:

According to Desouza et al. (2008), customers used to not be involved with business processes; customers' role was limited to consumption of the final products and services possibly giving their feedback to a company. Information technology has changed that drastically. For example, most airlines now allow passengers to book their tickets, choose their seats, print a receipt, and check in on-line. In addition, one of the outcomes of increased integration of customers into an organization's supply chain process is the "disintermediation" of certain players in the industry.[29]

The on-line booking of air travel resulted in disintermediation of travel agents, and hence increased the efficiency and effectiveness of the ticketing process.

What makes Apple the smartest technology company today is Apple's ability to move innovative ideas to commercialization quickly. The first to market wins in this competitive global market environment.

When you are the first company to market your products and services, you enjoy the first mover advantage. While your competition is releasing their initial products and services, you are making enhancements and upgrades. According to Adam DeGraide, a veteran internet marketer and sales guru asserts that Apple's iPad sold more than 300,000 units on day one, with more than one million apps downloaded and more than 250,000 eBooks downloaded. That was a lot of feet off the street.[30] Every competitor today in the global market wants to do business like Apple. Part of Apple's success is centered on discipline, focus, long-term thinking, and willingness to ignore the rules that govern everybody else's business. It's a strategy that is difficult to discern and tougher to imitate, but everyone wants to give it a try.[31]

Get in Line: Apple in Japan

Apple's exclusive iPhone partner in Japan SoftBank Corporation was aggressive in pushing iPhone sales in Japan. SoftBank is a telecommunication and media corporation in Japan with operations in primarily e-Commerce, internet, broadband and marketing. The success of iPhone has been contagious. The sale of iPhone in Japan by SoftBank has raised the company's profile and revenues to new highs as chronicled below:

2001: Apple's launch of the iPod in Japan raised SoftBank's profile to new levels. The hard drive music player successfully cuts into sales of Sony's MiniDisc and Discman players, which had long dominated Japan's portable audio market. It was evident that people took off work and others used their lunch hours to queue for the iPod in Japan.

2003: Japan's first Apple Store opens in Tokyo's Ginza District. Some 5,000 enthusiasts lined the street outside waiting for the opening.

2005: The iTunes Music Store Japan launched. Apple claims sales of 1 million tracks in the site's first four days.

2008: Apple rolls out the iPhone in July. Prospective customers began lining up outside the Omote-Sando SoftBank's Store in Tokyo five days before the phone goes on sale.

2009: SoftBank launched its "iPhone for Everybody" campaign in February, making the 8GB model essentially free to subscribers. According to GfK Group, one of the largest market research companies in the world maintained that in September of 2009, the new 32GB 3GS model became the month's best-selling handset in Japan.[32]

Challenges in Building Sustainable Innovation Programs

In today's competitive business environment, the ability of an organization to innovate is paramount. While most organizations have flashes or sudden burst of energy as a result of innovation, only a handful have been able to innovate on a continuous and sustained basis. Organizations facing disruptive innovation often exhibit incompetence and respond inappropriately to innovative opportunities. Their structures, routines, systems as well as policies and procedures that were tailored to existing operations prevent them from adapting to the quite different processes of calibrating inventions and turning them into innovations. They however, intent to invest in minor, incremental innovations that fit their current organizational design and structure instead of re-engineering and re-structuring their organizations to encourage innovation and change.[33] Several studies indicate that behaviors that hinder innovation are generally found in maturing organizations. Braganza, Awazu & Desouza (2009) report that as firms mature, they tend to become too comfortable doing what they normally do at the expense of innovative strategies. One distinguishing characteristics of Apple's leadership is that, they always try to get out of their comfort zone by enhancing their existing products and services, exploring new customer base and markets.

Braganza et al. (2009) maintain further that the comfort zones that maturing organizations create within their organizations may lead to myopia and most importantly may also hinder risk taking. Another behavior that may hinder organizations innovation programs may include their existing organizational structures, policies and procedures. The existing organizational structure, policies and procedures may become rigid over time hence encouraging only a narrow focus on operations and mission.

What makes Apple's organizational structure and mission unique from other technology companies is that Apple always remembers who they are and how far they've come within their industry. What makes some organizations less innovative and stagnant is that they lose the drive that got them where they are; they lose the creative energies, the openness to risk taking and experiments that allowed them to carve a niche and disrupt the incumbents when they first entered the market.[34] A case in point is Google's aggressive innovative programs designed to overcome Microsoft's organizational initiatives and strategies in the search engine industry. We will explore Google's aggressive innovative strategies in the next chapter. This doesn't mean Microsoft is less innovative and less aggressive in expanding its market niche; Microsoft is anticipating less customer demand and spending too much time in enhancing its existing products and services instead of innovating and developing new products and services. The most difficult challenge for Microsoft in the technology industry is that Microsoft fails to anticipate market niche. For example, Microsoft failed to anticipate the huge market for search in spite of Microsoft's huge financial outlay. Google on the other hand had anticipated a market niche in the search market and invested heavily to develop and make search capability available to its customers and clients.

Apple's takeover of the online music business with the invention of iPod is another example. Sony, the pioneer and inventor of the Walkman had the opportunity to lead the online music business but failed to do so because Sony's leadership focused only on improving its existing products and could not come up with an innovative product to integrate the online music business.[35] "As firms grow, they tend to exhibit common behaviors that prevent them from being adaptive to new environments, thereby limiting their ability to sustain their innovativeness" (Braganza et al. 2009, p.47). What challenges do organizations face in building sustainable innovation programs? Or what are the inhibitors of innovation?

Pursuit of Stability:

According to Braganza et al. (2009), some organizations today still create formal structures that are based on Taylor's principles. The silo structure, which group's people by expertise and the specialist work they perform. Organizations that achieve high levels of stability operate in a state of internal equilibrium. However, it's obvious that organizations do not exist in a vacuum; they have to thrive and survive in the dynamic and complex global market place in which stakeholders – customers, suppliers, regulators, and competitors – produce change every time they modify their expectations. Some organizations in the global market environment are too comfortable with their profit margins and are totally satisfied with where they are. Organizations that pursue stability often perceive disruptive innovations as threat; while strong competitors such as Apple perceives disruptive innovations as opportunity. "These differences in perception are important because they lead to debate over the best course of action to pursue. However, senior executives may procrastinate over taking decisions and allow energy-sapping in-fighting and turf wars to be waged at the expense of innovation and creativity" (Braganza et al. 2009, p.48). Pursuit of stability has hindered most organizations' initiative to disrupt innovation by developing products in anticipation of customer needs.

Risk Avoidance:

Multinational organizations that perceive eradication of risk as a strategy will be disappointed in the global market environment. According to Braganza et al. (2009), organizational risk cannot be eliminated; nevertheless, many organizations attempt to follow a risk avoidance strategy by making incremental changes even when the circumstances require radical changes. For example, for many years, IBM clung to the past by making incremental changes to its product lines, service proposition and market orientation. Increasingly, IBM became separated from its marketplace, customers and employees, until it took extraordinary effort of new leadership to make the innovative and breakthrough changes that IBM needed to compete again in the global marketplace. "Attempting to avoid risk by sidestepping the implementation of radical change is pointless. Organizations are more effective when they manage risk. However, in the face of disruptive technologies, it's critical to know which risks to manage. Three categories of risk require the close attention of incumbent organizations: people, process and knowledge" (Braganza et al. 2009, p. 48). Some organizations fail in the global business environment because they fail to take risks in entering certain industries. Enjoying first mover advantage is what organizations should pursue in their quest to survive and stay competitive; and more importantly to be perceived as innovative and creative.

Constrained By Experience:

The ability to change organizational mindset is an important strategic management skill. Some multinational organizations consistently hold onto certain core competencies that are no longer relevant in the global marketplace. Braganza et al. (2009) state the core competencies that created organizational success within a corporation may invariably become core rigidities that prevent the corporation from competing. Solutions that worked in the past may simply be irrelevant to the future. This emphasizes Apple's strategy of re-structuring and re-defining their mission and vision statements by breaking down corporate structures and empowering employees to anticipate customer needs and designing platforms to address those needs in a cost effective and timely manner. Constrained by experience can hinder an organization's ability to let go past core competencies that are non-value added to the organization. According to Braganza et al. (2009), while there is much discussion in the academic literature on corporate memory, little thought is given to corporate dementia; that is to say, the need for organizations to forget aspects of their past. Holding onto past glories can become a barrier to absorptive capacity, which describes the ability of an organization to recognize the value of new information, assimilate it, and apply it to commercial ends.

Apple's success has also been attributed to the fact that it has wakened up and let go past core competencies and business models that are not customer centered. Apple has re-designed its business model to utilize internal and external infrastructure to leverage the expertise and capabilities of their business partners in order to sustain their competitive advantage in the global marketplace. In an interview with Apple's senior executive he explained how Apple is pursuing expanded business and dropping product lines that are non-value added and more importantly streamlining and evolving new businesses that utilize their unique strengths in multimedia and the internet. The brief interview is shown below:

> The task in which Apple management and its Board of Directors is currently engaged in is to utilize Apple's strengths in order to position the Company for long-term strength and success. The most immediate and obvious work we must undertake is to quickly streamline operations in this tough economic times where people are losing their jobs in record numbers. We have also refocused our online services strategy away from a stand-alone proprietary business to one which uses and integrates with the Internet, which means we don't have to develop a costly infrastructure ourselves.
>
> Next, we have begun to develop strategies to fundamentally change our business model. In products, we

intend to simplify our product portfolio so our offerings focus primarily on innovative, differentiated and best-of-class products in our key market segments in education, business and the home. We are pursuing expanded business alliances to further promote and extend our platforms, evolve new businesses that utilize our strengths in multimedia and the Internet, and better manage our assets by leveraging the expertise and capabilities of our business partners.

Our goal is to ultimately redesign Apple's business so that we can carry out our most important strategic missions – anticipating customer's needs and designing platforms to exceed those needs. These include ensuring the continued superiority of our products and services especially in the areas of multimedia and the Internet; vibrant support from developers; the highest customer satisfaction and brand loyalty; leading positions in markets where Apple competes; and increased shareholder value.

Lack of Options:

Continuous improvement is key to organizational success. Some organizations get tied into the resources they have ignoring the fact that they need to explore other options to find better and effective ways of improving their operations. In today's competitive global marketplace, it's important to develop improved working methodologies and processes that are difficult to replicate by competition. Being satisfied with present resources and not trying alternative means to improve operations may hinder innovation and creativity. Apple's success is partly attributed to management ability to develop multiple innovative products and services by anticipating end users needs.

Legacy Systems:

Organizations are trapped with information and knowledge based systems they cannot get rid of because of the nature of information contained in those systems. The information contained in those legacy systems is obsolete but vital to the organization. Employees, suppliers, customers as well as other stakeholders are so connected and familiar with the systems in such a way that enhancing them to be innovative becomes a challenge and a major investment. If legacy systems within an organization are not properly managed, they may pose a tremendous hindrance to innovation and creativity. According to Braganza et al. (2009), the biggest challenge to organizations trying to innovate by overhauling their legacy systems is that, suppliers, employees and other stakeholders may resist change to the legacy systems because they are familiar with the systems and have better understanding as well as the shortcomings of the systems.

Employees, suppliers and other stakeholders may have developed routines to compensate the shortcomings. The introduction of new systems removes the certainties and more importantly creates high levels of anxiety as people have to learn about the new systems. Studies indicate that individuals within an organization have little motivation to implement technologies necessary to manage innovation. Apple has done a good job in this direction by designing their legacy systems to support innovation and future enhancements. Some U.S Government Departments and Agencies are notorious with legacy systems because of the difficulty and the resources needed to enhance and update them. The use of legacy systems has hindered most Federal, state and local governments' initiative to be innovative and efficient. McKendrick (2010) reports that even though various US government agencies and departments have been aggressively pursuing service orientation of their legacy systems, along with cloud, virtualization, and open source, to better integrate and manage their systems. Most Federal agencies have been struggling to keep their legacy systems updated and enhanced. For example, it is estimated that the US Secret Service needs about $187 million to update its legacy systems, but has only received $33 million so far from Congress through appropriations[35]. In designing new information systems to replace legacy systems, organizations must work collaboratively with their stakeholders to design and implement the new system in accordance with their stakeholders' needs and specifications.

Complex Power Structures:

Some organizations are troubled with complex internal structures and bureaucracy that hinders their ability to quickly move innovative products and services to commercialization. Apple's strength in leading the global innovation initiate is the ability to quickly move timely innovative products and services to commercialization. Complex power structures can tremendously hinder an organization's innovation and creative ideas. Complex power structures arise when it's difficult to make quick strategic decision within an organization. Braganza et al. (2009) asserts that overcoming the power and political structures within an organization requires strong leadership and clear single minded vision. Apple's CEO is a clear example of a strong leader with a single minded vision.

Power battles can blind people to innovations that are in their proverbial "grey space" or "white space." Grey space according to Braganza et al. (2009) represents innovations that are at the intersection of the capabilities of two groups. Grey space ideas often stimulate heated debates over which group will pursue them. Grey space innovations are often found in the public sector where two departments flash an idea about without either department taking ownership of it[36]. White space innovations however, represent innovations that do not fall under the responsibilities of any one group. Ideas in the white space never go anywhere as there is no enticing environment present for cooperation to thrive and a joint unit to take advantage of the opportunities[37]. According to Braganza et al. (2009), one large actuarial firm lost millions of dollars in business because neither the pensions nor the healthcare divisions took heed of global clients requesting products that provided their employees with an integrated package relevant to the employees' local situation. In today's competitive business environment, organization structures must be flattened or simplified to encourage rapid communication and management approval of certain key decisions made by employees. Employees must be empowered to make certain key decisions on behalf of their organizations without senior management approval.

Myopic Managers:

As organizations become established and more profitable, management may become narrow minded and the opportunity for cross functional collaboration and knowledge sharing become smaller. The effort to educate managers, executives, and employees about the significance and nature of innovation, its management and creation diminishes and this may hinder sustained competitiveness within an organization. It's natural for managers and executives to be myopic, however; to succeed in today's global competitive marketplace, managers and executives must combine knowledge across functional areas. Many managers are not trained in how to engage in such cross functional or interdisciplinary settings and hence cannot identify ideas from disciplines outside their areas of expertise. They also find it difficult to lead cross functional innovative teams[38].

Intervention to Innovation Inhibitors

In today's competitive global marketplace, it's almost impossible to avoid the inhibitors of innovation as outlined above; however, the aforementioned inhibitors must be properly managed from inception. Apple has been successful in managing novel ideas and more importantly has designed innovative ways of allocating resources to fund and manage innovation efforts within the organization. Apple's CEO and other senior executives have demonstrated the ability to resist temptation of investing only in areas that they have the know-how. Apple's CEO and senior executives are known for making innovative products even from by-products. It's important to take risks in every innovation initiative. Intervention to innovation inhibitors is summarized in exhibit 1 (adopted from Braganza et al., 2009).

Exhibit 1 – Interventions to Innovation

Intervention	Description
1. Use portfolio approach to allocate resources for innovation	Invest in traditional and novel products and markets
2. Train managers to be innovators	Distribute innovation competencies rather than leaving innovation in the hands of a few employees
3. Communicate the value of innovation	Explain the challenges and rewards of implementing innovative ideas
4. Revisit organization's mission	Align the organization's mission with the innovation policies
5. Governance of innovation	Dual power structures allow ideas to emerge from the bottom-up (decentralized power) and promote organization wide implementation (centralized power)

Apple's Strengths, Weaknesses, Opportunities and Threats

Some observers and Apple insiders agree Apple has some challenges and weaknesses that need to be addressed. Some observers and writers believe that Apple's total transformation from a niche player to a major consumer electronic company in the global marketplace depends on an effective solution of the following challenges. Apple's image will be tremendously enhanced in the global marketplace if Apple addresses these management challenges:

1. Inability to explore new markets within government and big businesses. Apple's market share within the government and big business is significantly low. Some observers and business writers believe that this is attributed to Apple's unwillingness to succumb to government pressures and demands because of Apple's business model which is only aggressive on consumers. It's easier to please consumers than the government or big business says Apple's senior executives. One senior executive acknowledged in a recent interview that government and big business sales or enterprise sales comprises only 10% of the computer market, while consumer sales comprises of 50%. Therefore, Apple has to do a better job in tapping into the potential huge market within government and big business.

2. Unhealthy business relationship with competitors. Some business writers see Apple's senior executives as overly arrogant and selfish. There is no doubt that this has adversely impacted Apple's profitability and image. Apple's prickliness deprives the company of untold business opportunities. Apple's revenues would have doubled if it had a good working relationship with its competitiors[38].

3. Inadequate product documentation. For the past several years Apple has not done a better job of clearly explaining certain complex parts of their products on their support page. According to consumers Apple makes certain sections look simple than is actually is. For example, the Airport Extreme or the Airport Utility Setting is widely mentioned as complex and difficult to set however, Apple failed to clearly explain this complex procedure on their support page. According to Martellaro (2010), Apple is run as a very lean organization, and when a new product phenomenon comes along like the iPhone or iPad, resources are diverted away from attending to details of previous technologies.

4. Business Transparency. Some business writers have exposed Apple's inability to explain its business activities to its end users as a public corporation. Apple has also failed to communicate the state of mind and the condition of health of its senior executives. For example, when Apple launches a product

or service, it doesn't inform consumers of its target market unlike other companies. It's important to inform end users the kind of market that your product intends to serve. According to Argenti (2009), loyalty must be built for the long term: A truly great company is much more than the sum of its innovative products and an addictive brand. Apple should not let the value and novelty of its assets expire nor should it let its goodwill flee. Lasting companies, which enjoy consistent success over the very long term, recognize that their most important assets aren't their product line or their bottom line but the strength of their relationships with core constituents such as end users, competitors and other stakeholders[40].

5. Inability to train future leaders within the organization. It's important for organizations to look within to replace senior executives. Apple has not designed a program to ensure that mid-level managers are properly trained to take up responsibilities of senior management.

6. Apple's refusal to disclose carbon footprint to the Carbon Disclosure Project (CDP). Every multinational organization is responsible for sustainable environment; and because of the importance of reducing carbon footprint with organizational products and services, most multinational organizations as part of their social responsibility initiative voluntarily discloses their environmental footprint to the Carbon Disclosure Project. The Carbon Disclosure Project is an independent non-profit organization holding the largest database of primary corporate climate change information in the world. The organization is headquartered in London with offices around the world. Thousands of businesses and corporations in the global market measure and disclose their greenhouse gas emission and climate change strategies through CDP. Apple has persistently refused to take the initiative to be involved in the activities of CDP.

7. Higher prices of products and services

Notable Strengths

1. Strong financial condition
2. Tremendous ability to empower, motivate and nurture talents within the organization

3. Tremendous ability to create innovative high quality products and services
4. Outstanding marketing and distribution strategy
5. Strong understanding of customer needs
6. Passion for excellence
7. Strong desire to enter new markets
8. Amazing ability to delegate effectively to mid level managers
9. Significant investment in R&D
10. Outstanding customer loyalty
11. Strong product differentiation

Weaknesses

Apple continues to find itself in the middle of crisis where its contractors and subcontractors are accused of unethical business conduct. There were reports of employee suicides and forced labor in many manufacturing plants where Apple equipment was assembled. Even though there were series of negotiations between Apple and the contractors to address those issues, there are reports of occasional violation.

Notable Opportunities

1. Penetrating other market segments such as online social networking industry and video card industry
2. Working collaboratively with competitors to develop products and services
3. Acquiring competitors
4. Huge market opportunity in South-East Asia
5. Being more environmentally friendly by disclosing carbon footprint
6. Strong global demand for computer application and software
7. Strong global demand for state-of-the art communication devices

Some Threat

1. Rapid technological changes
2. Cheaper substitutes
3. Copyrights infringement
4. New entrance

Summary

Innovation will not be effective if management does not consistently communicate its value and purpose to employees. It's important for management to communicate the value of innovation to employees. Management must not just communicate the value and purpose of innovation to employees; they must encourage it by empowering employees, investing on their development and education as well as rewarding them accordingly for their innovative ideas. To be competitive in today's global marketplace, organizations must re-visit their mission and vision statements to align them with innovation policies and procedures. Encourage employees to think outside their respective functional areas. Management must remember that solutions that worked in the past may not be relevant for the future survival of their organizations. According to Braganza et al. (2009), organizations that do not continuously reinvent themselves are bound to become extinct. Apple and its senior executives have realized the importance of reinventing themselves and their organization by re-structuring and re-organizing their mission statements to align them to innovation policies and procedures.

In this chapter I examined the strategies Apple uses to stay as the number one most innovative company in the personal computers and mobile communication industry. I explored Apple's marketing and innovation strategies. I reviewed the basics of value innovation as well as the blue and red ocean strategies. I explored the inhibitors of innovation as well as the journey and sources of innovative ideas. Apple's tremendous success in the mobile communication industry is mostly attributed to its ability to manage knowledge. Apple is able to identify, absorb, acquire and utilize external and internal knowledge to its advantage. Apple's strengths, weaknesses, opportunities and threats have been examined.

Endnotes

1. Adams, R., Bessant, J., and Phelps R (2006). International Journal of Management Review, 8(1), 21-47; pp38.
2. http://www.businessweek.com/interactive_reports/innovative_50_2009.html
3. http://www.businessweek.com
4. http://www.apple.com
5. http://www.businessweek.com
6. Spirrison, B. (2010). Steve Jobs on the New iPhone and How it began with the tablet
7. http://www.apple.com

8. Senge, P.M. (2004). Learn to innovate. Know your purpose and assess your results. Executive Excellence, 21(6) pp3.
9. Apple Inc., 2009 Annual Report
10. Apple Inc., 2009 Annual Report
11. Apple Inc., 2009 Annual Report
12. Apple Inc., 2009 Annual Report
13. Apple Inc., 2009 Annual Report
14. Kim, W.C., & Mauborgne, R. (2005). Blue Ocean Strategy – How to Create Uncontested Market Space and Make the Competition Irrelevant, Boston: Harvard Business Press.
15. Kim, W.C., & Mauborgne, R. (2005). Blue Ocean Strategy – How to Create Uncontested Market Space and Make the Competition Irrelevant, Boston: Harvard Business Press.
16. Leavy, B. (2010). Design thinking – a new mental model of value innovation. Strategy and Leadership, 38(3), 5-14.
17. Leavy, B. (2010). Design thinking – a new mental model of value innovation. Strategy and Leadership, 38(3), 5-14.
18. Marcus, A. A. (2010). *Management Strategy: Achieving Sustained Competitive Advantage.* New York: McGraw-Hill Irwin.
19. Kim, W.C., & Mauborgne, R. (2009). Blue ocean strategy. Leadership Excellence, 26(5).
20. IBM (2006) Global CEO Survey. Business Model Innovation – the New Route to Competitive Advantage. Retrieved September 4, 2010 from: http://www-935.ibm.com/services/uk/cio/flexible/enflex_wp_business_model_innovation.pdf
21. Baloh, P., Jha, S., & Awazu, Y. (2008). Building strategic partnerships for managing innovation outsourcing. Strategic Outsourcing: An International Journal, 1(2), 100-121.
22. Baloh, P., Jha, S., & Awazu, Y. (2008). Building strategic partnerships for managing innovation outsourcing. Strategic Outsourcing: An International Journal, 1(2), 100-121.
23. Baloh, P., Jha, S., & Awazu, Y. (2008). Building strategic partnerships for managing innovation outsourcing. Strategic Outsourcing: An International Journal, 1(2), 100-121.
24. Baloh, P., Jha, S., & Awazu, Y. (2008). Building strategic partnerships for managing innovation outsourcing. Strategic Outsourcing: An International Journal, 1(2), 100-121.
25. Baloh, P., Jha, S., & Awazu, Y. (2008). Building strategic partnerships for managing innovation outsourcing. Strategic Outsourcing: An International Journal, 1(2), 100-121.
26. Baloh, P., Jha, S., & Awazu, Y. (2008). Building strategic partnerships for managing innovation outsourcing. Strategic Outsourcing: An International Journal, 1(2), 100-121.
27. Desouza, K.C., Awazu, Y., Jha, S., Dombrowski, C., Papagari, S., Balor, P., & Kim, J.Y. (2008). Customer-driven innovation. Research Technology Management
28. Fogg, I., Husson, T., Mulligan, M., & Wiramihardja, L. (2010). Competing With Apple: Assess Capabilities, Not Intent, To Benchmark Competitors or Potential

Partners. Retrieved, September 6, 2010 from: http://www.forrester.com/rb/Research/competing_with_apple/q/id/56396/t/2

29. Desouza, K.C., Awazu, Y., Jha, S., Dombrowski, C., Papagari, S., Balor, P., & Kim, J.Y. (2008). Customer-driven innovation. Research Technology Management, p35-44.

30. DeGraide, A. (2010). Leaning from Apple. Rough Notes, 153(6), 106-107.

31. Monjoo, F., Caplan J. (2010). Apple Nation. Fast Company, 147: p69.

32. Schwartz, R. (2009). Apple of their eye. Billboard Research Library, 121: 47.

33. Braganza, A., Awazu, Y., & Desouza, K.C. (2009). Sustainable innovation is challenge for incumbents. Research Technology Management, p46-56.

34. Braganza, A., Awazu, Y., & Desouza, K.C. (2009). Sustainable innovation is challenge for incumbents. Research Technology Management, p46-56.

35. McKendrick, J. (2010). Report: 1980s legacy systems continue to plague some US government ops. Retrieved October 1, 2010 from http://www.zdnet.com/blog/service-oriented/report-1980s-legacy-systems-continue-to-plague-some-us-government-ops/4178

36. Braganza, A., Awazu, Y., & Desouza, K.C. (2009). Sustainable innovation is challenge for incumbents. Research Technology Management, p51.

37. Braganza, A., Awazu, Y., & Desouza, K.C. (2009). Sustainable innovation is challenge for incumbents. Research Technology Management, p51.

38. Braganza, A., Awazu, Y., & Desouza, K.C. (2009). Sustainable innovation is challenge for incumbents. Research Technology Management, p51.

39. Martellaro, J. (2010). The five problems Apple faces. Retrieved September 9, 2010 from: www.macobserver.com

40. Argenti, P. (2009). Lessons from the Apple/Jobs Controversy. Access Intelligence.

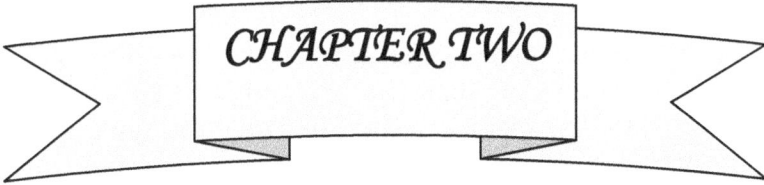

2 – Why Google is Considered Number Two Most Innovative Company

S ustainability is important for growth and long-term success in today's workplace. "Sustainable development will not happen without innovation. There is growing acceptance that to move towards sustainability there must be changes in the ways in which business operates and in the products and services it provides. The challenge for business is to develop innovation strategies that respond to increasing environmental and social pressures, and thus consider the needs and expectations of a wide array of stakeholders."[1]

Chapter Learning Objectives

- Thorough understanding of what Google is doing different in the global market place to sustain its competitive advantage.
- Exploring Google's innovative information access platform, products and services.
- Understanding Google's competition and what impact they have on Google.
- Comprehending why Google is still the preferred search engine in spite of competition.
- Recognizing how Google is managing innovation.
- Understanding how organizations can guarantee the relevance of their products and services.

- Recognizing Google's weaknesses in executing its innovative strategies.

Introduction

Innovation has no handbook or manual – from the words of the dynamic and most popular Apple senior executive. I have explored the amazing technological and innovative initiative of Apple in Chapter One and why Apple continuously wins the title as the number one most innovative company in the global marketplace. I have also examined some innovative marketing strategies Apple has adopted to stay competitive in the personal computer and mobile communication industry. It's difficult in the global marketplace for one company to dominate the creation of innovative products and services. Apple has demonstrated that it's possible for one company to do so. Chapter one examined how Apple has been able to sustain its competitive advantage in the global marketplace by illustrating this with key interviews with senior executives and experts. We learned in Chapter One that spending billions of dollars in R&D doesn't make you an innovative organization. In a 2006 IBM survey of CEOs of multinational organizations, R&D was ranked eighth as a source of innovative ideas. Employees were ranked the top most significant source of innovative ideas. This explained why Apple has been successful in commercializing most of its innovative ideas. In 2009 Apple spent $1.3 billion in R&D with market capitalization of $185.5 billion while Google spent $2.8 billion in R&D in the same year with market capitalization of $172.4 billion[2]. Apple spends money in the continuous development and training of its workforce, has a workplace environment that nurtures creativity and innovation.

Continuous employee training and development is key to sustaining competitive advantage. In addition to continuous employee training and development, it's important for organizations to communicate the value and purpose of innovation to employees across all functional areas. Organizations must re-visit their mission statements in order to align them with innovation policies and procedures. Innovation and creativity must be encouraged and rewarded organization-wide. In Chapter One, we gained an elementary comprehension of value innovation, blue and red ocean strategies as well as the journey and sources of innovative ideas. We recognized the importance of customer driven innovation in Chapter One; we also examined the challenges organizations face in building sustainable innovation programs or innovation inhibitors. Solutions were offered to address the innovation inhibitors. Finally, Chapter One discussed some weaknesses that Apple faces in executing its innovation strategies.

Chapter two will examine why Google is considered number two most innovative company in the global market environment in a case study format. Google's success story can be traced back to the importance of college and graduate school projects. Google was born as a result of a school project. It's evident that some multinational organizations came into being as a result of school project; Google's success story is beyond school project. Often what is required to make progress in technology is focus. You cannot make progress in the competitive field of technology if you are distracted. Who would have thought in 1998 that anyone could get for free a high-resolution picture of their house from above, and even from the street? That's Google Earth, Maps, and Street View. Finding important technological areas where progress is currently slow, but could be made fast, is what Google is all about[4]. Google's ultimate goal is to create a perfect search engine for its end users. Search ads continue to be the primary source of revenue for Google.

Google's growth is much attributed to its aggressive acquisitions and partnership with competitors. With online advertising, Google remains the most dominant advertiser in the global market environment. The organization uses multiple innovative technologies to target end user interests: this enables Google to help other organizations design marketing programs to target those end user interests. Roughly 70% of Google's resources are allocated to core search and advertising, and the organization has been doing a tremendous amount of work on each of those key areas. According to one of the founding members, search is a really hard problem. In order to do a great job in helping people find answers, you would need to understand global information and the exact meaning of each and every query requested by end users. End users expect perfect answers instantly and this is where Google utilizes its outstanding innovative tools to respond instantly by providing real time answers to end users.

No one understands global languages more than Google. "We have dramatically improved our understanding of all the different languages, the meanings and synonyms of words, and the many different types of specialized information such as businesses and products. We continue our effort to extract more and more real meaning from the web in order to help people find the right answers."[5] With Google's recent innovative technology called Google's translate, you can translate instantly any major spoken language in the world – you can search and read results of languages you do not speak. End users have realized the efficiency of this innovative technology. This technology is being incorporated into YouTube so that end users can watch videos even if they don't speak similar language.

Approximately eight years ago Google entered the enterprise market with its Google Search Appliance to target large organizations, educational institutions, the Federal, state and local governments. This technology enables organizations to automate their document files for easy access and retrieval. Document retention and management has been a major challenge for both public and private organizations. Google docs, an innovative system to help individuals and organizations manage their files online had great reviews from end users. Google docs enable individuals and organizations to store and backup their files of any type online. This may eliminate the need for carrying flash drives or thump drives for some business people. The distinguishing feature between Google docs and other document management systems is that Google docs is very collaborative, meaning it enables document editing, uploading, controlled document sharing, data collection capability and more importantly, enables open form of data export in a variety of formats.

In the area of diversification and corporate social responsibility, Google announced a few years ago an experimental project to build an ultra high speed broadband networks in communities across the country to serve about 50,000 to 500,000 people. The access would be about 100 times faster than most people have in their homes. Communities and individuals were asked to submit ideas to Google as well as their support for the experimental project. Google received overwhelming support and response to that initiative. The most widely publicized response was the one submitted by the Mayor of the city of Topeka, Kansas. For the month of March 2010, the Mayor named the city after Google. According to one Google senior executive, the response of the city of Topeka indicated how communities are in dire need of better and faster internet access.

Google Corporation Case Study – What Google is Doing Different

"Sergey and I got over our fears of failure and finally founded Google in 1998. If we had known then what Google would become in 2009, we would have been totally flabbergasted. The scale and scope of our services, and the opportunities they offer users, are phenomenal, and we are very lucky to be a part of this business. Rather than try to run through an exhaustive list of everything we have done this year, I'm going to focus on a couple of issues – access to information and a new model of computing – that are of particular interest to me, and on which I have unique perspective."[6] Google Inc., co-founder Larry Page, in 2009 Annual Report.

Overview

Google is a global technology leader focused on improving the ways people connect with information. Google started as a school project in 1996 and became a legal entity in 1998. Founded by Larry Page and Sergey Brin; Google is headquartered in Mountain View, California and was reincorporated in Delaware in 2003. The organization has over 19,835 employees worldwide with revenues of $22.7 billion; R&D expenditure of $2.8 billion and a market capitalization of $172.4 billion.[7] The organization's innovations in web search and advertising have made their web site top internet goodwill as well as the most recognized name in search technology in the global marketplace. Google's mission is to organize the world's information and make it universally accessible and useful. Google has three main categories of end users:

1. Users: The first category of Google's customers or end users is users. Google provides this category of end users with products and services that enable them to more quickly and easily find, create, and organize information that is useful to them.
2. Advertisers: The second category of Google's customers or end users is advertisers. Google provides this category of customers with cost effective means to deliver online and offline ads on television across the organization's sites and through Google Network. Google Network is a network of online and offline

third parties that use their advertising programs to deliver relevant ads with search results and content.

3. <u>Google Network Members and Other Content Providers</u>: The third category of end users is Google network members and other content providers. With this category of end users, Google provides online and offline collaboration with its AdSense programs. This includes the various ways Google distributes it AdWords ads for display on web sites and television. Google AdWords is an automated online program that enables advertisers to place targeted text based and display ads on Google websites as well as on the network members'.

Google's Information Access Platform, Products and Services

Google's core business relies on the capability of its founders in exploring traditional business areas where lack of technology is hindering growth. For example, to succeed in today's competitive business environment, business leaders must be able to understand the language and culture of the markets they serve. Google has been able to address this issue with its innovative tool called Google Translate. Google Translate can instantly translate between any of the 54 major languages built into this innovative tool. In addition, business leaders can search the tool and read results in languages they don't speak. Google re-evaluates these traditional businesses by incorporating modern technology to enhance growth and profitability. Google's strength and opportunities rely primarily on the numerous languages spoken on the global market place. The organization innovates to find ways and means to connect people as well as provide them with the information they need to get connected instantly.

Google's innovative search engine has revolutionalized information access for students, researchers, business people, analysts, and the academia. Google's Universal Search tool provides information to end users in multiple formats. Universal Search tool has taken online marketing and product sales to new highs. Organizations that use this tool enable them to provide goods and services to potential customers as if they are in the actual store. For example, instant product information, news about the product, videos of the product, price, and price comparison are instantly available to potential customers. One interesting thing about Google's Universal Search tool is that it costs nothing to organizations if no one buys the products and services they advertise on Universal Search. In other words, it's made available to organizations on cost per acquisition basis. Organizations pay a fee to Google if customers buy. Interest based ads are another innovative tool Google invented to target customers with particular interests. With the interest based ads, customized ads are sent to a particular group of consumers with distinct interests. For example, interest based ads can be sent to pet lovers, soccer fans, college professors, teachers, union members and what have you.

1. Google Analytics: This is one of Google's innovative ads tools used to help organizations track returns on their ads investment. When organizations have large marketing budgets, they will like to know whether the budget is worth increasing or decreasing. To better understand how a particular ad worked for an organization, Google Analytics helps organization determine if they need to change, edit or drop a particular ad within the organization. Traditional ads tools do not provide this kind of flexibility. This is an ad measuring tool designed to help organizations control their ad or marketing budgets.

2. Google Geo: A practical application of this global innovative tool arose in the tragic earthquakes in countries like Haiti and Chile. With the help of this innovative tool, Google Geo was utilized to gather and process updated high resolution 3D imagery of all possible tragedies like devastated buildings and casualties on the streets of Haiti and Chile. Google Geo has made it possible for people to be at different places at a time. Very useful tool for relief organizations like the Red Cross as well as the broadcast industry. Streets, homes, buildings, street addresses and other objects can be viewed around the world with the use of this innovative tool. In the 2010 soccer Olympic in South Africa, a significant number of people used this tool to view surrounding streets, the stadia and restaurants around each and every area that the games were played.

3. Google Books: "It is truly a dream fulfilled for me that we now have 12 million books scanned and available for searching at books.google.com. That is already bigger than almost any university library, and we're not done yet. I am very excited about the possibilities to help expand human knowledge, create

new revenue streams for content creators, and improve the quality of search for every Google user."[8] This is an amazing invention. The innovation engine has over 137 years of human knowledge in the form of books, magazines, articles and what have you. Google Books is an innovation system designed to capture past and present knowledge in a form of books, magazines, and articles for online readers and researchers. This system was designed in collaboration with major publishers around the world.

4. Google Trends: This tool provides end users the ability to track the popularity of keyword searches over time on Google website. End users can type in a keyword in Google Trends including names of individuals around the world to determine the relative search interest or the popularity of such keywords and names of individuals.

5. Google Scholar: This is a great tool for researchers and students seeking peer reviewed papers, theses, books, abstracts, and articles. Google Scholar enables end users to search for scholarly articles in journals such as Journal of Management, Harvard Business Review, Academy of Management Executives, Strategic Management Journal and many others.

6. Google Music Search: This tool enables users to type in an artist name, album, or song and plays the song instantly; or access public review of the album before playing it.

7. Google Finance: This tool enables users to have an instant review of market performance. Stock prices, news events, data and financial charts.

8. Other Products and Services: All of Google's products and services cannot be mentioned in this book. However, the above are the most revenue generating products and services for the organization.

Google's Competitors

Google faces tremendous competition from every aspect of their business especially from organizations that seek to connect individuals with information online as well as provide them with advertising and product information. Google faces competition from the following organizations:

1. <u>Yahoo Inc. and Microsoft Corporation's Bing</u>: Bing is a search engine like Google developed by Microsoft in 2009. Bing enables users to find and organize answers they need to make informed decisions in a timely fashion. According to Murphy (2010), even though Google faces serious competition from online search and advertising, Google still rocks the charts as the global top search destination. But according to new numbers from Hitwise, an online analytics service, there's been little change from August to September of 2010 in terms of the percentage of users who access the Big Three search sites— Google, Bing, and Yahoo. This indicated that Google is still a wee shy of capturing three-fourths of the entire online search market at 72.15 percent for September of 2010. Google is still dominating its rivals by a pretty healthy degree."[9] Yahoo managed to stay distant second in the search rankings with 13.5 percent of all U.S. searches—roughly one-fifth of Google's presence. Bing.com search engine trailed a distant third, grabbing a mere 10.1 percent of all online searches. But, to Microsoft's credit, searches powered by its Bing engine (Yahoo and, obviously, Bing.com) ranked 23.6 percent of the market. That's nearly one-third of Google's share."[10] This is a healthy competition for end users considering Microsoft's financial strength. The competition among Google, Yahoo and Bing indicates that, in the global marketplace experience is irrelevant, what matters is innovation, consistency and timely commercialization of innovative products and services.

2. <u>Vertical Search Engines and e-Commerce sites such as WebMD (for health searches), Kayak (travel searches), Monster.com (job searches), and Amazon.com and eBay (e-commerce)</u>: Google has strived beyond these organizations because Google takes innovation and creativity seriously. Google's open culture nurtures creativity and encourages dialog. In addition to having a corporate environment that nurtures creative thinking, Google employees are all equity holders with significant collective employee ownership. This connects employees' well-being to the success of the organization. Employees' well-being increases as the organization succeeds.

3. <u>Social Networks, such as FaceBook, Yelp, or Twitter.</u> Studies indicate that some end users rely on social network sites such as FaceBook and Twitter for product referral instead of utilizing traditional search sites such as Google. This poses a tremendous challenge to Google's competitiveness. In spite of all the social network sites and what have you, Google is still rocking the charts as the global top search engine.

4. <u>Television, Radio, Newspaper, Magazine, Billboards, and Yellow Pages Ads.</u> These are the traditional forms of ads that Google still competes with. Television and radio especially Television remains Google's key competitor. According to a recent study by Ball State University on the media consumption habits of average Americans, despite the Internet's steady rise in popularity over the last few years, television remains the dominant medium in most U.S. households. On average, the general population spends over four and a half hours a day in front of the tube, making TV watching one of the most common modern leisure activities. Is it any wonder then that television advertising is also the form of advertising?   Advertising on television allows organizations to show and tell a wide audience their business, product, or service. Television allows organizations to actually demonstrate to households the benefits of their products and services."[11]

5. <u>Mobile Application Providers</u>: The providers of mobile applications have also been directing customers away from the traditional search engines. The provision of car rental companies, restaurants, places of entertainment and what have you on mobile phone applications threaten the traffic on Google's applications.

Why Google is Still the Preferred Search Engine in Spite of the Competition?

In spite of Google's size of nearly 20,000 employees, the organization still maintains its small company flavor. It's common to see almost everyone eating in the company's café. The organization's commitment to creativity and innovation primarily depends on each and every individual being comfortably and freely sharing ideas and opinions with senior management. According to Chalhoub (2010), innovation process is a people process whereby formal systems and processes are not prerequisites to technological innovations. Participative style with open communication leads to increased performance in the long run. The more employees participate in planning, organizing, and decision-making, the more they feel eager to contribute ideas. Participative style enhances the way criteria are set in evaluating the innovativeness of an individual or a group of individuals within the organization.[12] Google's culture of open communication amongst employees and senior executives have always increased the creative minds and aggressiveness of employees across all functional areas; creative minds of anticipating end user needs and designing appropriate solutions ahead of time to address those needs. The reasons why Google's mission of organizing the world's information and making it universally accessible and useful still dominates the global search engine technology are as follows:

Relevance: When end users query the Google search box, their query is sent to Google's applications which compare the query with all documents stored in their index to identify the most relevant matches. Within seconds, Google applications prepare a list of the most relevant pages and also identify the relevant sections and bits of text, images, videos and what have you. What end users get back is a list of search results with relevant information extracted beneath each results. This is not common in most search engines. End users get exactly what they've asked for. With Google's innovative technology, personalized results are provided based on end users search history. Relevance as a competitive advantage means you get exactly what you've asked for.

Comprehensiveness: Comprehensiveness as a sustained competitive advantage means when end users query Google's applications for answers, the answers are returned with integrated images, videos, news, books and what have you into the single search. Google has index of billions and billions of web pages and their index is approximately 100 million gigabytes.

Freshness: Google is still the most preferred destination for search because of the real time information that Google provides to end users. Google search can provide end users with information within seconds of its publication. Freshness of information here means the real time information that Google provides its end users.

Speed: In a recent nationwide poll about one single thing in the office or at home that is annoying. 90% of participants responded slow network connection and information retrieval. Google's average query response time is approximately one-fourth of a second. This is almost instant considering the comprehensiveness and relevance of the query results. With Google's innovative technologies called auto-complete, most of the time end users query sentences and phases are completed even before they finish typing their sentences or phases and the results follow instantly.

How Google is Managing Innovation

"With intensifying competition and evolution in management thought, entrepreneurial behaviors are increasingly becoming a focal point in evaluating a company's performance in the market. Performance innovation needs to be managed at the organizational level by planning, setting policies and guidelines, specifying targets and standards, and reviewing periodically individual and collective performance."[13] Innovation is complex and very ambiguous. Difficult to manage and has no single definition. However, according to the United Kingdom Department of Trade and Industry (DTI), innovation is the successful exploitation of new ideas.[14] How does Google exploit new ideas? Google exploits new ideas by effectively managing the following models and concepts:

1. Inputs: According to Adams, Bessant, and Phelps (2006), inputs management is concerned with the resourcing of innovation activities and includes factors ranging from finance, to human and physical resources, to generation new ideas[15]. For example, Google is testing vehicles that drive themselves to help improve road safety as well as address environmental concerns. So far, the self-driving cars have traveled more than 140,000 miles in experiments. In addition, Google has recently announced its initiative to invest in clean energy superhighway. This clean energy superhighway will generate power from offshore wind farms to 1.9 million homes without overtaxing the already congested mid-Atlantic power grid. Google would invest as much as $5 billion to create a 350 mile long network of underwater cables stretching from northern New Jersey to Virginia. This initiative will eliminate the need for offshore

wind developers to build transmission lines of their own. Google is partnering with Good Energies, an environmentally focused international investment company, to find the project[16]. An organization's innovation initiative is dead without consistently generating ideas and managing inputs. Ideas are the raw materials for innovation and Google is full of them.

2. Knowledge Management: Google manages innovation by effectively managing knowledge. Knowledge absorption or management is an organization's ability to identify, acquire and utilize external knowledge critical to its existence. Knowledge management is also concerned with obtaining and communicating ideas and information that underlie innovation competencies, and includes capability and networking[17]. Google has taken knowledge management to new levels by providing instant answers to the wondering mind. What can't you get from Google's search engine? From Google Maps, Word Processing, Email, Tools for publishers, mobile ads and what have you. To survive in the global market today as an organization, you must constantly generate meaningful ideas and work to simplify and commercialize those ideas. In addition to simplifying and commercializing those ideas, the ideas must be communicated to all those who need to know. Central to this perspective is the idea of absorptive capacity that is an organization's ability to absorb and put to use new knowledge, and involving an ability to recognize the value of new, external knowledge, assimilate it, and apply it to commercial ends[18].

3. Innovation Strategy: Innovation strategy generally defines an organization's innovation policies and procedures. Organizational practices must be aligned with innovation practices. In other words, organizational mission must be redefined to include innovation policies and procedures. Innovative ideas may be hindered within an organization if employees do not see the value and purpose of it. Innovation is a tradition and culture within Google. Google's commitment to innovation depends on each and every employee being comfortable sharing and communicating ideas across functional areas. Because of Google's commitment to innovation, no

employee is hindered from communicating ideas directly to senior executives.

4. Organizational Culture and Structure: According to Adams et al. (2006), organizational culture and structure concern the way employees are grouped and the organizational culture within which they work. The perceived work environment, comprising both structural and cultural elements does make a difference to the level of innovation within an organization. Google is very aggressive and inclusive in their hiring process. Google favors ability over experience. Diversity and innovation is Google's business. The philosophy of inclusiveness and diversity is what lays the foundation for Google's innovation. Never judge a search engine by its interface. Behind that simple search window is one of the most complex technology infrastructures in the world. The complex technology infrastructure is run by equally diverse group of people. Google doesn't just accept difference; Google thrives and accelerates on difference. Senior executives support this initiative for the good of their workforce, products, and the community in which they live[20]. The success of Google's organizational structure and culture in supporting innovation has been well documented in academic literature.

Several measuring instruments have been developed by many researchers and management writers to test organizational climate that supports innovation process. The most widely cited instrument is the Team Climate Inventory developed by Anderson and West (1996 and 1998). The Team Climate Inventory can be used to explain a large part of the variance in team's innovative performance[21]. The Climate Inventory instrument was developed around four fundamental factors: The first factor is Participative Safety – this explains how involved and participatory each and every team member is in the decision making process and how psychologically secure each team member feels about proposing new and improved methodology of achieving results. Second factor is Support for Innovation – this factor explains senior executives support for innovation and how they communicate innovation across functional areas. Innovation initiative in every organization is viewed as a top down approach; innovation initiative would be hindered if it has no senior executive support.

Third factor is Vision – how attainable are your innovation initiatives; are they clearly defined and shared across functional teams? Are they attainable? Google senior executives always ensure that their innovation process is clearly articulated in their vision statement as well as broken down into manageable segments for all teams to understand and implement. For example, the announcement of Google's free mobile operating system called Android that powers millions of smart phones and the testing of vehicles that drive themselves to help improve road safety and address environmental concerns. Also, the announcement of clean energy superhighway are a few examples of Google's vision statements that articulate how to attain innovation projects both in the short and long run. The fourth factor is Task Orientation – task orientation is the commitment of teams to achieve the highest possible standards of task performance, including the use of constructive progress monitoring procedures[22].

5. Portfolio Management: The importance of portfolio management to successful product innovation has recently emerged as a key theme in academic literature. Portfolio management is important because of the rapidity at which resources are consumed in the innovation process and the need for these to be managed[23]. Bard, Balachandra and Kaufmann (1988), maintain that an organization's competitive advantage in the global market environment is primarily dependent on how the organization manages its pool of talent workforce and its R&D portfolio. To excel in the quest for innovative products and services, it's important for organizations to do uncommon things in the global market place.

Google had done uncommon thing for the first time by launching a trading floor in the Stock Market to manage its $26.5 billion in cash and short term investments. The initiative was the third-biggest cash pile among tech companies after Microsoft and Cisco Corporations. The objective was to effectively manage its portfolio which was conservatively managed[25]. As part of Google's portfolio management initiative, the organization built a state-of-the-art cash-management system to improve returns and to manage its liquidity[26].

6. Project Management: Project management is concerned with the processes that turn inputs into a marketable innovation. The innovation process is complex and dynamic consisting of multiple of events and activities. Some activities and events can be identified as a sequence while others may occur concurrently. It is evident that innovation processes may differ to some extent across functional areas within organizations on a project-by-project basis[27]. According to Adams et al. (2006), several studies have made the effort to measure project management efficiency, mostly in the form of comparisons between budget and actual project costs, project duration and revenue forecast; however, have found out that the only measure of project management success is speed. The researchers add that innovation speed has been positively correlated with product quality or the degree to which the product satisfies customer requirements. The way Google manages and launches its innovation projects is phenomenal. Google uses the stage-gate process, the phased development, product and cycle-time excellent as well as total design project management tools to effectively manage its innovation projects to commercialization.

To demonstrate how Google effectively manages its projects, Google has developed multiple project management application software for project managers. Project management application software such as Google Wave the most notable, is a live shared space on the web where project managers can discuss and work together using richly formatted text, photos, videos, maps and what have you to help manage their respective innovation projects. One important aspect of a successful project management is communication. Several studies have demonstrated the existence of positive correlation between internal communication and innovation. According to Adams et al. (2006), internal communication facilitates the dispersion of ideas within an organization, it increases diversity and more importantly contributes to team climate. External communication is also important because it focuses on whether communication is happening the way it should. For example, always ensure customers, suppliers and other external stakeholders are informed of the innovation process and documented.

7. Commercialization: Commercialization is one of the critical stages in the process of innovation management. Commercialization is the end product of innovation; and several studies indicate that most innovative ideas or products do not get to this state because of the complexity of innovation management. Several activities are carried out in this stage. The most significant activity in this stage is marketing – that is sales, distribution, joint ventures, market investigation, compliance, market testing, promotion and so on[27]. Some organizations seem to pay little attention to this stage hoping the product or service will sell itself. Organizations need to invest more in this last stage of innovation management. Google's innovation management strength relies on its ability to effectively market its innovative products and services. Google carries most of its sales and marketing activities in professional conferences it organizes annually.

Google also utilizes its own technology to advertise its products and services. In 2007, 2008, and 2009 sales and marketing expenses as a percentage of revenues were 8.8%, 8.9% and 8.4% respectively[29].

How to Ensure Your Products and Services Are Relevant Today and Tomorrow?

It's naïve on the part of global business managers to assume that their products and services will be relevant today and tomorrow. Business managers will be surprised to find out how much valuable information their employees and customers hide from them. How do you ensure as a manager that valuable product and service information is not hidden from you and that your product and or service will be relevant today and tomorrow?

1. To ensure your product and or service is relevant today and tomorrow, do not rest on your laurels. Management must encourage employees to think outside the box and more

importantly, management must be open to new ideas. Incremental innovation must be the long term strategic initiative of management to ensure that their products and services do not become irrelevant. Incremental innovation must be the long term strategic initiative of management because incremental innovations can provide business leaders the ability to gain new customers while increasing the income generated by existing customers. It also offers the ability to capture customers by offering a broad array of differentiated brands within important core categories. Business leaders may use incremental innovations to respond to radical industry wide changes by adding value and product differentiation[30].

2. Has any employee or senior management suggested any improvement to your product and or service within the last five months? Senior management must encourage employees across functional areas to frequently report customer experience both positive and negative. Product support must not be left to a group of employees. Product support must be an organization wide initiative. Senior management must encourage every employee especially front line employees to tell them the inconvenient truth about their products and services. Employees must be encouraged to report undistorted information from customers – what they like and dislike about their products and services and what they hope to see changed. Lack of candor can have an insidious effect on a company; especially when front line employees suppress information and distort communication with their bosses, the problem repeats itself up the line. Those with the power to set priorities and allocate resources end up with significant distorted view of the customer experience.[31] To ensure that your product and or service remains relevant, you must constantly incorporate customers experience into your product and or service. Continuously ask customers what they want to see different in your product or service.

    Google's success in online advertising and technology emanates from continuous collaboration with customers – welcoming both positive and negative feedback from customers and working innovatively to capture those feedbacks to enhance product and service usefulness.

3. What is your promise to your customers? Is it well known to every employee? Organizations are bound to lose significant revenues and make their product or service irrelevant if the organization's promise to customers is not well understood by employees and senior management. Everyone in an organization needs to know what they their organization's promises and then make their best efforts to deliver that promise. If the promise is too vague, not relevant to most customers or not understood internally, it may have significant negative impact on the present and future offering of the product or service[32]. For example, every employee within Google understands that Google's promise to its customers is to provide relevant, comprehensive and fresh answers to customers when they type their questions in the search box. The promise of relevance, comprehensiveness and fresh doesn't end there; the promise is complete when the information is delivered at the highest speed possible – usually within seconds. This promise is well understood by every employee across the functional areas.

4. Have you made any significant improvement in your product or service in the past 24 months? Have you incorporated any new ideas into your product or service within the past 24 months? The most successful outcomes occur within an organization when the organization genuinely meets customer needs in radically new ways[33]. Google is notoriously known for radically meeting its customer needs by continuously enhancing its products and services in a quarterly basis. This enables Google to make its products and services more relevant to its end users. Continuous innovation is the engine that drives highly successful organizations; it's an especially potent competitive weapon in tough economic times like today because it enables organizations to redefine the market environment in their favor in order to achieve the needed growth and profitability[34].

Google's Notable Weaknesses

In spite of the tremendous success and innovative capability of Google; the organization is not without challenges. Google will remain the top five most innovative organizations if management pays attention to the following issues: I will leave some of them for further discussion:

1. Product Awareness. Google is significantly challenged in carefully making its new inventions known to end users in a timely manner. Some end users have to figure out Google's new inventions or had to stumble on them without much direction or guidance. Google focuses most of its resources in resolving design and engineering problems at the expense of resolving end user problems.

2. Inadequate Monitoring of Click Fraudsters. Google has been unable to drive click fraudsters out of business in spite of technology enhancements to do so. Click fraud occurs when a user intentionally clicks on a Google AdWords ad displayed on a web site for a reason other than to view the underlying content. Fraudsters use specialized technology to drive business away from Google advertisers. This could lead the advertisers to become dissatisfied with Google's programs, which has led to several ligations and loss of revenues in recent years[36].

3. Eliminate offline ads and focus on online ads which are the core business of the organization.

4. Extensive diversification. Google must stay focused and innovate more to expand its core business.

5. Copyright infringement with authors.

6. Compromise of end user privacy. The Federal Government has passed several legislations to combat the abuse and misuse of personally identifiable information. Google has not shown much effort in combating the misuse of personally identifiable information of its online customers.

7. Inadequate intellectual property enforcement.

8. Insufficient resource allocation for healthcare projects. Google is weak in the promotion and maintenance of healthcare supplies because of its lack of experience in this area and has not yet acquired any organization with healthcare management as core business area.

9. Lack of product integration

10. Poor customer relation. Google has no published customer service numbers where customers can talk to a live person for help. Even though most Google products and services are self

served, there must be a call center to handle the needs of desperate end users who are interested in talking to a real voice instead of a recorded voice.

11. Over reliance on network members for a significant portion of their revenues. The loss of these network members could adversely impact Google's profitability[37].

12. Inability to manage growth.

13. Inability to monitor index spammers. Google has been unable to control the activities of index spammers on their innovative search engine. This is one of the primary weaknesses that Google needs an innovative technology to address. Index spammers manipulate web searches of Google users by ensuring that web results are irrelevant to users.

Summary

Google means "every." However, Google operates in a universal space. The organization is not trying to sell to your customers; it's trying to send your customers to the most important web sites based on their queries. If you deliver more information than any other organization, then you are exactly the kind of site that Google wants to send people to. Google's recognition is built upon how well it matches end users with the information they are looking for. Organizations can wholeheartedly join Google in enhancing their own reputation by giving Google a genuinely great place to send customers[38]. "Google recognizes that everything is a commodity except the information. The computer, its chips, user interfaces, internet services, and everything else can be copied by a competitor. Given advances in technology, there is always a disruptive innovator around the corner who will be able to build a better product.[39]" No one has been able to build that better product so far to outpace Google. Creating a global relationship with customers is not easy. It's being a challenge for most organizations in the global market environment to create such an outstanding online relationship with customers. Google's innovative capability and strong financial resources has made the organization the envy of its of competitors.

I have discussed Google's organizational initiative and overview, explored the innovative information access platform, products and services. I have Examined Google's competitors in the global market place; and why Google is still the preferred search engine in spite of the amazing competition the organization faces. I have also discussed how Google is managing its innovative strategies and how to ensure that your products and services are relevant in the eyes of the customer today and tomorrow. Finally, I have examined some notable organizational weaknesses within Google.

Endnotes

1. Ayuso, S., Rodriguez, M.A., & Ricart, J.E. (2006). Responsible competiveness at the micro level of the firm using stakeholder dialogue as a source for new ideas: a dynamic capability underlying sustainable innovation. Corporate Governance, 6(4), 475-490.
2. Apple & Google Inc., 2009 Annual Reports
3. Google Inc., 2009 Annual Report – Founder's Letter
4. Google Inc., 2009 Annual Report
5. Google Inc., 2009 Annual Report: pp-i
6. Google Inc., 2009 Annual Report
7. Google Inc., 2009 Annual Report
8. Google Co-founder - Sergey Brin in 2009 Annual Report
9. Murphy, D. (2010). Google Dominates U.S Search Market for September. Retrieved October 9, 2010 from: http://www.pcmag.com/article2/0,2817,2370521,00.asp
10. Murphy, D. (2010). Google Dominates U.S Search Market for September. Retrieved October 9, 2010 from: http://www.pcmag.com/article2/0,2817,2370521,00.asp
11. AllBusiness (2010). Television Advertising Pros and Cons. Retrieved October 10, 2010 from: http://www.allbusiness.com/marketing/advertising-television-advertising/2592-1.html
12. Chalhoub, M.S. (2010). Innovation management and thought leadership – A cultural requirement in a global competitive environment. The Journal of American Academy of Business, 16(1), 240-245.
13. Chalhoub, M.S. (2010). Innovation management and thought leadership – A cultural requirement in a global competitive environment. The Journal of American Academy of Business, 16(1), 241.
14. DTI (1998). An Audience With Innovation: Innovation in Management. London: Department of Trade and Industry.
15. Adams, R., Bessant J., & Phelps, R. (2006). Innovation management measurement: A review. International Journal of Management Reviews, 8(1), 21-47.
16. Google Casts a Wide Net – Cover Story (October 13, 2010 issue of Express New Paper, p.9). Retrieved October 13, 2010 from www.expressnightout.com

17. Adams, R., Bessant J., & Phelps, R. (2006). Innovation management measurement: A review. International Journal of Management Reviews, 8(1), 21-47.
18. Adams, R., Bessant J., & Phelps, R. (2006). Innovation management measurement: A review. International Journal of Management Reviews, 8(1), 21-47.
19. Ramanujam, V., and Mensch, G.O. (1985). Improving the strategy – innovation link. Journal of Product Innovation Management, 2(213-223).
20. Google (2010) Corporate profile. Retrieved October 17, 2010 from: www.google.com
21. Anderson, N., and West, M.A. (1996). The team climate inventory: development of the TCI and its applications in teambuilding for innovativeness. European Journal of Work and Organizational Psychology, 5(53-66).
22. Anderson, N.R., and West, M.A. (1998). Measuring climate for work group innovation: development and validation of the team climate inventory. Journal of Organizational Behavior, 19(235-258).
23. Adams, R., Bessant J., & Phelps, R. (2006). Innovation management measurement: A review. International Journal of Management Reviews, 8(1), 21-47.
24. Bard, J.F., Balachandra, R., and Kaufmann, P.E. (1988). An interactive approach to R&D project selection and termination. IEEE Transactions on Engineering Management, 35(139 – 146).
25. MacMillan, D. (2010). Google's Latest Launch: Its Own Trading Floor. Retrieved October 17, 2010 from: http://www.businessweek.com/magazine/content/10_23/b4181033582670.htm
26. Schuller, M. (2010). Google Takes Over Wall Street? Portfolio Management Ahead. Retrieved October 17, 2010 from: http://www.market-melange.com/2010/05/29/google-a-new-portfolio-manager-in-town/
27. Adams, R., Bessant J., & Phelps, R. (2006). Innovation management measurement: A review. International Journal of Management Reviews, 8(1), 21-47.
28. Calantone, R.J., and Benedetto, C.A. (1988). An integrative model of the new product development process: an empirical validation. Journal of Product Innovation Management, 5(201-215).
29. Google Inc., 2009 Annual Report: pp-46.
30. Fisher, J. (2007). Incremental innovations. NPN, National Petroleum News, 99(5), pp46.
31. Barwise, P., and Meehan, S. (2010). Is your company as customer-focused as you think? MIT Sloan Management Review, 51(3), 63-68.
32. Barwise, P., and Meehan, S. (2010). Is your company as customer-focused as you think? MIT Sloan Management Review, 51(3), 63-68.
33. Barwise, P., and Meehan, S. (2010). Is your company as customer-focused as you think? MIT Sloan Management Review, 51(3), 63-68.
34. Rothaermel, F, T. (2010). Innovation strategies combined. MIT Sloan Management Review, 51(3), 13-15.
35. Boulton, C. (2006). Google Watch. Retrieved October 23, 2010 from:

http://googlewatch.eweek.com/content/google_strategy/top_5_google_weaknesse s.html

36. Google Inc., 2007 Annual Report, p.20.
37. Google Inc., 2007 Annual Report, p.25.
38. Smith, R. (2010). Google means every. Industry Research Institute Inc., pp: 67 - 69.
39. Smith, R. (2010). Google means every. Industry Research Institute Inc., pp: 68.

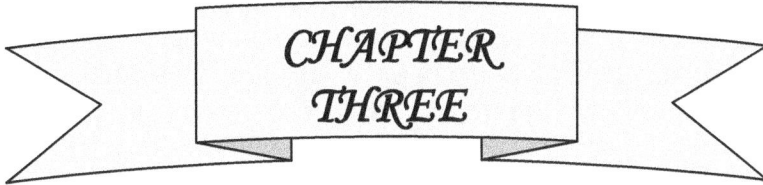

3 – Why Toyota is Considered Number Three Most Innovative Company

V alue creation is essential for success in today's competitive workplace. "No matter what the business, Toyota will never slow the pace of technological development that drives its future growth, or of the productivity improvements that keep it competitive. For a company to grow, its employees must grow, and we will continue to strengthen our on-site, hands-on experience as well as our encompassing approach to manufacturing; that results in added value for all stakeholders. By doing so, we will not only become more competitive, but I believe we can also lay the foundation of a strong, new Toyota that will lead the global automobile industry forward into the future."[1]

Chapter Learning Objectives

- Comprehending what Toyota is doing different in leading the hybrid automobile industry.
- Understanding the meaning of innovation within Toyota.
- Exploring why Toyota is considered a learning organization.
- Realizing how Toyota is building quality into processes.
- Gaining elementary comprehension of the components of innovation ecosystem within Toyota.
- Evaluating Toyota's strengths, weaknesses, opportunities, and threats.

Introduction

According to several consumer reports, Toyota brands remain the most reliable automotive brands in the global marketplace. Toyota's fundamental mission is to make better cars and contribute to society. The organization has overcome numerous challenges in its quest to accomplish this mission. Some of the challenges include labor disputes, emission controls and oil crises, trade liberalization, trade friction as well as the recent global financial crises. The global financial crises has not only impede Toyota's growth and stability but has forced many multinational organizations into bankruptcy and financial chaos. In spite of the impact of the financial crises on Toyota and on other corporations, Toyota has managed to stay focused on its core mission and vision of putting the customer first and making better cars and to contribute to the well-being of the society. Product and market oriented management teams have been formed to strategically design and market products that meet and exceed the needs of customers in each global market. Toyota has never compromised quality and affordability. Before a vehicle moves into the assembly plant, affordability and quality are the fundamental components that are thoroughly evaluated by all individuals and teams across functional areas. Quality and affordability are re-evaluated at every stage of production to ensure the customer can afford the product and service.

To address the needs of its customers' worldwide, Toyota product and market oriented teams are tasked to build networks and to offer a full lineup of vehicles for all the communities it serves. The networks cover over 170 countries and regions worldwide. Toyota's regional vision was created to recognize that each and every region is at a different stage of economic development, with the regional vision in mind, high quality products and services are customized to meet the needs of customers in each region.

Intelligent Transport System (ITS) is a business area that Toyota is seriously exploring to further improve road safety. Toyota is continuously exploring this technology to support safe driving so that traffic accidents of the future can be prevented effectively than the existing safety technologies. Information technology and telecommunication is another business segment Toyota has integrated into its products to set it apart from competition. This groundbreaking technology involves the integration of vehicles and cell phones;

enhancing the convenience and comfort of cars with car navigation system technology to include Bluetooth Audio, which will allow the playback of songs that have been downloaded on a cell phone. This innovative technology will enable customers to enter a destination by transferring location data obtained from a cell phone. As part of Toyota's non-automotive manufacturing initiative, the organization entered into housing construction in 1975 to construct high durable and earthquake resistance housing with built in security systems, health and environmental features. "In 2009, we began sales of environment-friendly homes with a heat loss coefficient of 1.86 Q-value, which has one of the highest levels of thermal insulation in the homebuilding industry."[2] Toyota has also started developing Home Energy Management Systems which are designed to reduce utility costs and the environmental impact.

Marine business is another segment Toyota is actively involved in. Toyota builds and sells pleasure boats for its wealthy end users. The organization also builds marine engines and a host of marine components by utilizing the organization's advanced innovative technologies. Toyota is deeply involved in the biotechnology and afforestation segments. As a result of Toyota's biotechnology and afforestation initiative, the organization contributes immensely toward resource recycling in the society. Forest restoration models have been built across countries to help save the planet.

Toyota Case Study – What Toyota is doing to Stay Innovative and Unravel Competition?

Toyota Motor Corporation is the largest multinational automotive and non-automotive corporation headquartered in Japan. The organization was founded by Kiichiro Toyoda in 1937. Toyota North America was founded in 1957. Toyota builds vehicles and parts at a dozen plus plants in North America. The organization invested more than $18 billion in its North American operations, since its inception in 1957. Toyota North America is the fourth largest auto maker in North America employing 8 percent of Toyota's global workforce throughout the U.S. and Canada; producing more than two million cars and trucks annually. Statistics indicate that the organization is more competitive in automotive manufacturing than in non-automotive business. Toyota Motor Corporation's has global employees of 320,590. Toyota's non automotive business segment includes housing, financial services, communications, GAZOO, marine vehicles, biotechnology, afforestation and what have you. The GAZOO segment provides visual vehicle information network through the internet for Toyota customers.

According to the International Organization of Motor Vehicle Manufacturers, automobiles are a liberating technology for people around the world. Personal automobile allows people to live, work and play in ways that were unimaginable a century ago. Automobiles provide access to markets, to doctors, to jobs. Nearly every car trip ends with either an economic transaction or some other benefit to our quality of life. The automobile industry is also a major innovator, investing over $200 billion in research, development and production. The auto industry plays a key role in the technology level of other industries and of society. Vehicle manufacturing and use are also major contributors to government revenues around the world, contributing well over $900 billion annually[3].

How Toyota Is Oiling Its Innovation Engine?

As the global economy is yearning to reduce gasoline consumption and to reduce the impact of its emission into the environment, Toyota has answered this call through its aggressive innovative initiative by being the first global organization to design and produce hybrid automobiles for the global economy. Some global business leaders have been asking management writers and researchers thought provoking questions such as: can the organizational structure of a company contribute to the acceleration of the innovation management in the spirit of fast innovation? Why is it that Toyota is the first global automobile producer to innovative, design and produces the first hybrid automobile? "The capacity to learn and build knowledge greatly enhances the likelihood of continuing success. While innovation can occur by serendipity, sustainable innovation, from which collaborative and competitive advantage emerge, needs a systemic and effective management approach based on knowledge and learning."[4]

Continuous acquisition of knowledge and learning is what drives Toyota's innovation engine. In addition, Toyota has created conducive organizational environment for free flow of knowledge and knowledge transfers. Organizational structure can tremendously contribute to the acceleration of innovation management in the spirit of fast innovation. Toyota has demonstrated this concept in its corporate philosophy designed to foster a corporate culture that enhances individual creativity and teamwork value, while honoring mutual trust and respect between labor and management and more importantly, pursue growth in harmony with the global community through innovation management.[5]

The Hybrid Innovation Technology

The hybrid innovation technology within Toyota began in 1993 with a simple question designed for the innovation team: "Can vehicles in the upcoming twenty-first century remain the same as they have been up to now?" Hybrid innovation technology was difficult to gasp during the 90s. Toyota innovation team worked diligently to simplify the concept of hybrid to the man on the street. Toyota innovation team launched an aggressive research into the kind of vehicle that would be best for the twenty-first century. A vehicle that will be friendly to the environment with high design quality and affordability was the driving force of the hybrid technology. The hybrid innovation technology was also designed to achieve three main objectives: 1) improve fuel efficiency in order to reduce Co_2 emissions, 2) make exhaust emissions cleaner in order to lessen atmospheric pollution and 3) respond to energy diversification. Based on the design technology, the hybrid was designed to operate on gasoline and bio-ethanol or hydrogen.

The scope of the hybrid innovation was expanded to include areas such as ease of boarding and existing, body size, design, fuel efficiency as well as societal and environmental issues.[6] Prius is the symbol of Toyota hybrid innovation technology. Prius is a Latin word meaning "to go before" – designed to answer the ultimate environmental question where automobiles, the earth and people and live symbiotically. The first generation Prius was launched in 1997 while the second generation Prius was launched in 2009. While Toyota's competition is trying to design their first generation Prius-like automobiles, Toyota is working to enhance its third generation Prius. This is a competition gap that cannot be easily filled. According to Toyota's Executive Vice President – Product Management and Research Development – "in addition to strengthening and advancing the environmental and safety technologies that are two of Toyota's greatest strengths, I will take on the challenge of creating vehicles that are truly exciting and fun to drive."

Toyota's hybrid innovation technology is the first of its kind among global automobile manufacturers. Toyota has diligently sought harmony among people, society, and environment, and more importantly contributes to the sustainable development of society via its innovative and creative manufacturing processes. Since the organization's foundation, it has continuously worked to make a difference in the sustainable development of society through provision of innovative and high-quality products and services that lead the times.

Toyota As a Learning Organization

The best companies are those that always make developing internal talent a high priority. Since organizations need talented individuals to buy into their vision and bring the vision to fruition, organizations need to track top talents in order to sustain their competitive advantage in the global market place.[7] No wonder Toyota implements one million ideas within a year. Where does Toyota get the ideas from? The ideas are generated internally from its talented workforce. Toyota's competitive advantage is derived from its fundamental principle as a learning organization.

There are no managers in Toyota. Toyota only has trainers and learners. "Dynamic learning organizations are built and maintained by servant leaders who lead because they choose to serve."[8] Senior executives at Toyota don't talk the talk; they walk the talk by ensuring that every employee is fully developed to maximize their capabilities. Maximizing employees' capabilities is what brings about creativity and innovation because they are fully developed intellectually and emotionally to handle complex issues. A common saying that is often heard among senior executives and trainers around Toyota is that "we do not just build cars; we build people." Every new product development program, every prototype, every quality defect in the factory floor, and every kaizen activity is an opportunity to develop people.[9] Effective employee development is not a new concept in business, it is found in almost every organization's policy handbook and manual however, the interesting question to ask is how many organizations are actually ensuring that their workforce is fully developed?

Toyota's innovation capability is based on five basic principles which are closely associated with learning organizations. It may have been difficult for Toyota to sustain its competitive advantage in automobile manufacturing without the following five basic principles.

1. According to Senge (1997), learning organizations embodies new capabilities; these new capabilities are what propel Toyota to the top of their industry. Language and communication is considered important component in Toyota's quest to become competitive and innovative. Within Toyota, language acts as an instrument for connection, invention, and collaboration. According to Senge (1997), when language and communication is the primary component of an organization's strategic management, it enables individuals within the organization to talk from their hearts and connect with one another in the spirit of dialogue. Their dialogue weaves a common fabric and connects them at a deep level of being. When people talk and listen to each other in this manner, they create a field of alignment that produces tremendous power to invent new realities in conversation, and to bring about these new realities in action.[10] Because individuals within Toyota can freely talk from their hearts and connect with one another easily, they always have an inquiring mind into complex issues and always analyze issues from systems thinking perspective.

2. Leadership has a different connotation within Toyota. Toyota's leadership has been able to address key fundamental questions within their organization to ensure that every employee has right level of tolerance for change as well as the right mind to be creative and innovative. The basic question that has been addressed to ensure every employee within Toyota is ready for change is, and I urge every business leader to address this simple question in their organizations and see what happens. The question to address is: what particular challenges do you face in implementing change in your organization? Do you find employees flexible and willing to change? Why do you think this is the case? [11] Business leaders can divide and conquer this question by further breaking it down into segments such as: What is hindering employees to change? – is it lack of communication? Is it lack of knowledge? – is it lack of training?

And what have you. If each of these questions is thoroughly addressed, employees will be more flexible to accept change and more importantly open their creative and innovative minds. The second direct innovation question that must be addressed to guide and direct the minds of employees to certain obsolete business processes that need to be addressed includes the following; because, equipping employees to be innovation minded cannot be overemphasized in today's competitive global market place: Business leaders must closely address these questions: Can you clearly describe your organization's vision for innovation? Within your organization, what will innovation produce, enhance, or make obsolete? What processes and practices do you have in place to encourage innovation? Who are your innovation leaders within your organization? Where is innovation occurring within your organization? [12] These are the basic questions that Toyota leadership has thoroughly addressed to ensure that their workforce understands the organization's vision for innovation, what business processes the organization needs to eliminate or improve and more importantly to develop the workforce to implement and easily accept change.

Delegating more to its well trained and talented employees and giving up control to the workforce is what is propelling Toyota's innovation engine. Toyota's workforce believes that their trainers or leaders are committed to their well-being and that they can freely make critical decisions on behalf of their leadership. "It has been proven in military campaigns that the only leader whom soldiers will reliably follow when their lives are on the line is the leader who is both competent and whom soldiers believe is committed to their well-being."[13]

3. The third basic principle that propels Toyota's innovation engine is that, leaders ensure learning arises through performance and practice. Toyota's policy of giving employees the opportunity to learn on the job has tremendous positive impact on employees' development and creativity. Toyota's management calls this the philosophy of genchi genbutsu or monozukuri – meaning learning from the source or on-site, hands-on experience. Returning to the roots of the monozukuri

philosophy that have nurtured Toyota since its founding, we are striving to create a new automotive paradigm - one that contributes to a bountiful society as it helps preserve the Earth's environment.[14] This was a remark of Toyota's Chairman Fujio Cho as he emphasizes on the importance of monozukuri's philosophy to the success of the organization. Toyota's philosophy of monozukuri and genchi genbutsu is closely related to Ancient Greeks philosophy that to be successful in any field of endeavor, three things are necessary – nature, study, and practice. Practice is key here because management should not assume that what employees have learned will be put into practice; management must ensure that what employees have learned is put into practice.

4. The fourth principle process and content of innovation must not be separated. Toyota doesn't improve segmented policies and strategies without addressing the fragmented and competitive relationship among the managers who formulated the strategies and policies.[15] Individuals who have brainstormed or generated the innovation ideas must be part of the implementation.

5. The final principle is forgetting the notion of unknown. Innovation always leads business leaders to the field of unknown and most business leaders are nervous about the unknown. Toyota practices transformation learning because the organization is not scared of failure. Fear of failure is what hinders some organizations from implementing innovative and creative ideas. At a point in time Toyota will sponsor employees to learn concepts that are unrelated to their duties and responsibilities. Robust organizations provide their employees with not only the necessary room for innovating outside of their duty areas, but also the necessary resources to explore auxiliary areas.[16]

How Toyota Is Building Quality into Processes?

The notion of building quality into processes is found in an internal document known as "Request Regarding Inspection." This document was developed in the 60s to address the influx of insufficiently trained new employees in the assembly plants. Product quality was seriously hampered due to insufficient training for the newly hires. There was the need to develop a document to help ensure quality at the assembly lines. Some senior executives in Toyota believed at the time that the idea behind an inspection is to eliminate the need for inspections. The executives believe further that as long as standards in processes could be kept at the highest possible levels, inspections in all the assembly plants may not be necessary. It may be difficult to keep standards at the highest possible levels in segments of the organization; because of that quality building processes are put in place to ensure highest possible quality.

Toyota is building elegant solutions to optimize product quality and reliability. According to May (2006), elegant solutions demand optimizing quality, cost, and speed. These are the three primary drivers of customer value in all goods and services. Taken together, they separate leaders from followers.[17] Toyota automobiles are considered the highest quality and reliable automobiles in the global market place because of the philosophy of Total Quality Management which is enshrined in all fabric of the organization.

With the concept of TQC, all employees within the organization are required to regard the next processes on the production line as their customers and provide them with the required amount and quality of goods and services in a timely manner. Quality control circles will study ways to identify causes of product defects when they occur and will determine counter-measures to prevent re-occurrence. High product quality, low cost, durability and reliability are what are sustaining Toyota as the top innovative organization in the automobile industry.

There is a simple explanation as to why Toyota is considered the most successful automobile producer in the automobile industry. Toyota success story is hard to replicate because of Toyota's ground-level innovation engine. The innovation engine ignites perfection. According to May (2006) Toyota's assembly floor employees may implement over a dozen ideas per shift. Trainers or managers may spend over half their time on a portfolio of ideas and projects. By the time a competitor will figure out what Toyota is doing, the innovation team is already equipped with the right tools to change the course of the innovation process or enhance it in a way it has never being done before. Toyota is conducting research and development for cutting-edge technologies in various fields to provide appealing products and services that meet or exceed the needs of customers around the world. The organization is also engaged in research and development to provide vehicles that offer comfort and the highest level of safety for its global customers.

Innovation Ecosystem in Toyota

How does Toyota capitalize on organizational investments in human capital and research? In other words, how does Toyota deliver the fruits of research and development through product creation? Toyota does this through innovation ecosystem. What is innovation ecosystem? According to the National Research Council – Committee on Comparative Innovation Policy, innovation ecosystem captures the complex synergies among a variety of collective efforts involved in bringing innovation to market[18]. Toyota brings innovative products and services to market in a timely fashion by investing heavily in customers, research and development, employees, business partners, shareholders, the environment and in communities around the world.

How Toyota Invests in Customers

Toyota is committed to excellence in manufacturing in order to provide state-of-the art high quality automobiles at affordable prices to their customers. Toyota does this by aggressive cost cutting initiative at the production floor. Toyota's promise is to continue to focus on the challenge of making better cars that are appealing to customers in the global markets. Part of Toyota's investment in its customers is the constant interaction with them to ascertain what they need and how they need it. Toyota's technological strength does not recline on its ability to develop vehicles through innovative technologies, but also in the tight integration of its Group companies in every global market that help to understand and process customer needs in a timely fashion. In addition, Toyota holds events in every global market to help customers understand the constantly changing performance and features of cars. These customer events cost significant amounts of money to manage.

In these customer events, everyone, from children to adults, experience the joy that cars offer. Toyota also carries events and activities to help its dealership staff broaden their knowledge of Toyota's products and services. China and other emerging markets in Asia and Central South America promise to become a strong engine for the future growth of Toyota. It's evident that China's economy as a whole is potentially as large as the U.S market; however, Toyota needs a different business model to fully penetrate the Chinese market. The organization is establishing a business model that will enable them to visualize things from customers' perspective and more importantly will enhance the business model as the market grows. As the Chinese market grows, Toyota will introduce competitive models that will meet customers' needs in timely fashion. For the rest of Asia, South America as well as other areas, Toyota's share in certain areas is still low and more aggressive growth initiative is warranted in the future. Toyota provides multi-purpose vehicles to over 140 countries worldwide including South Africa, Argentina, Asia and others. Toyota also manufactures high quality vehicles that can ride the waves of regional motorization. This includes the provision of vehicles that can be rated alongside the innovative international multipurpose vehicles.

How Toyota Invests in Research and Development Activities

To ensure efficient progress in research and development activities, Toyota invests aggressively in coordinating and integrating all phases, from basic research to forward-looking technology and product development. With respect to such basic research issues such as energy, the environment, information technology, telecommunications, and materials, Toyota's projects are regularly reviewed and evaluated in consultation with outside experts to achieve efficient research and development cost control. Cost control at the production floor is what is sustaining Toyota's competitive advantage. Effective cost control is a strong innovation ecosystem within the organization. "The overriding goal of Toyota's technology and product development activities is to minimize the negative aspects of driving, such as traffic accidents and the burden that automobiles have on the environment, and maximize the positive aspects, such as driving pleasure, comfort, and convenience. By achieving these sometimes conflicting goals to a high degree, we want to open the door to the automobile society of the future[19]."

In fiscal year 2009, Toyota's research and development expenditures totaled approximately $450 billion worldwide[20]. These expenditures represented 4.4% of the organization's worldwide revenues. The organization works closely with its suppliers to develop parts and components more efficiently because efficient and equality components make a quality car. Toyota commitment is to continue to make substantial investments in research and development involving forward-looking, cutting edge or leading edge technologies as well as the development of products and services related to the environment, energy, and more importantly safety. The organization's pledge to its customers and shareholders is to ensure that these ecosystem investments will be essential in preserving their competitive advantage in terms of technologies, products and services.

How Toyota invests in its Employees as part of Ecosystem Innovation

"The best companies are those that always make developing internal talent a high priority.[21]" According to Rose, Kumar and Pak (2009) organizational learning is more of a need than a choice at the present time; it is almost impossible to notice organizations that will admit ignoring learning, since this would be akin to be accepting the start of its demise[22]. Any organization that ignores learning, employee development, and technological innovation will be forced out of business. Toyota has a huge worldwide budget for its employee training and development. The organization's recognizes the importance of workforce training and development. Developing internal talents has been Toyota's strategic management initiative since its formation. The organization respects its employees and understands that the success of their business is led by each and every individual's creativity and good teamwork across functional areas. As part of ecosystem innovation, Toyota stimulates individual employee growth and development. In addition, the organization supports equal employment opportunities, diversity and inclusion as exemplified in its management structure.

Toyota strives to provide fair working conditions and to maintain a safe and healthy working environment in order to nurture innovation and creativity. The most important aspect of this ecosystem innovation initiative is that the organization respects and honors the basic fundamental human rights of its worldwide workforce; in particular, the organization does not use, support or tolerate any forms of forced or child labor which is apparent in some large multinational organizations. Through effective communication and dialog, Toyota builds and shares the value of mutual trust and mutual responsibility and more importantly works together to sustain the competitive advantage of the organization for generations to come. Fostering ethical behaviors among management and leadership of the organization is key to the long term survival and profitability of the organization.

How Toyota is investing in Business Partners as a form of Ecosystem Innovation

One of the success stories of Toyota is that, the organization invests so much in its business partners such as suppliers and dealerships. The organization believes that the success of its business partners directly translates to its success. For example, Toyota spends millions of dollars annually in special events to broaden the knowledge of its worldwide dealers to better understand the technology behind the organization's products and services. In addition to the annual training and development for its suppliers and dealers, the organization respects and works closely with each of them through a long term relationship to realize mutual growth based on mutual trust. Toyota maintains free and fair competition in accordance with the laws and regulations of the country it does business worldwide.

How Toyota is investing in its Shareholders as form of Ecosystem Innovation

According to Kaur and Narang (2009), corporate management has been placed under growing pressure to implement financial strategies that create value for its shareholders. Although maximizing shareholder wealth has become a paramount corporate mission. They add that how this mission is to be achieved is much less certain. For many years, company executives and shareholders have relied to standard accounting ratios, such as Earnings Per Share, Return On Investment, Return On Equity and what have you as the best criterion for evaluating shareholder wealth. However, there has been a growing awareness that these traditional accounting measures are not reliably linked to increasing the value of a company's shares. Kaur and Narang (2009) maintain that this occurs because earnings do not reflect changes in risk factor, nor do they take account of the cost of equity capital. So, the conclusions drawn on the basis of such measures are sometimes far from reality Kaur and Narang (2009) added. The researchers stated as part of their conclusion that the substantial way through which companies can create value is to earn sufficient economic returns to its shareholders[23].

In a similar study, Lombard (2002), holds that maximizing shareholder value is the essential outcome of any transaction. However, finding the right key to unlocking value is often strewed with pitfalls and dangers that are always obvious – even to those with the sharpest business acumen. Lombard (2002) adds that businesses can increase chances of success if they can identify the "hard keys" which open the door to value realization as well as "soft" keys which can access the enormous potential of an organization's people and culture[24]. Lombard (2002) defines hard key as due diligence, synergy evaluation and integration of planning on the part of organizations in unlocking organizational value for shareholders. However, the researcher defines soft key as management decision as to how the organization will be managed, resolving cultural communication and cultural issues within an organization[24].

Toyota management understands the soft keys and hard keys in unlocking shareholder value as well as measuring shareholder wealth. Since its inception, Toyota has earned enough economic value to reward its shareholders. Due diligence and vigilance is the fundamental guiding principle across Toyota's global business operations. The organization strives to enhance corporate value while achieving stable and long term growth for the benefit of their shareholders. Toyota provides its shareholders and investors with timely and fair disclosures on their operating results and financial conditions worldwide.

How Toyota is contributing to the Environment as Part of Ecosystem Innovation

Toyota aims for growth that is in friendship with the environment. The organization achieves this by striving to minimize the environmental impact of its business operation worldwide. Toyota is working diligently to reduce the effect of vehicle operations on climate change and biodiversity. The organization develops, establishes, and promotes technologies enabling the environment and the economy to coexist harmoniously. As part of the organization's guiding principle, Toyota seeks to build lasting relationship and cooperation with a wide group of individuals, profit and non-profit organizations involved in environmental preservation initiatives.

Toyota's Investment in Communities/Societies around the World as part of Ecosystem Innovation

Corporate reputation refers to publics' collective opinion of an organization over time. It's important for an organization to maintain a positive goodwill in the communities they do business. A positive goodwill enhances an organization's ability to attract and retain employees. Many management consultants and researchers maintain that an organization's goodwill or reputation can have a tremendous impact on the organization's ability to retain talented employees. A positive reputation also enhances corporate branding, enabling a company to use its brand equity to launch new products and enter new markets. Reputation can positively affect financial performance, institutional investment, and share price over time[25].

The subject of poor corporate management and governance through bad leadership has become a topic of discussion among management consultants and lawmakers around the world. In recent years, global lawmakers have been critical in strengthening corporate regulations to ensure business leaders make sound ethical decisions in their strategic management initiatives. We have all witnessed in recent years how dysfunctional or immoral leaders can damage the welfare of corporate stakeholders. Corporate social responsibility is a general concept concerning what is judged to be good or ethical about corporate behavior[26]. To ensure long term growth in the global market place, organizations have to earn the respect and trust of the communities in which they do business. Simply contributing to the well-fare of the communities is the enough. Organizations have to demonstrate good corporate citizenship by making ethical business decisions in addition to their socio-economic contribution. Toyota has several committees that are tasked with monitoring corporate business activities in relation to ethical business decision in all the communities that Toyota operates.

Honoring the culture, customs, history and laws of each community that Toyota does business is a fundamental business principle within Toyota. The organization constantly searches for safer, cleaner and superior technology that satisfies the on-going needs of the respective communities for sustainable mobility. Toyota does not tolerate bribery by any business partner, government agency or public authority. The organization maintains honest and fair relationship with government agencies and public authorities around the world or in communities it does business.

Development of World's First Rear-Seat Center Airbag

Toyota innovation team always works hard to ensure they produce award winning vehicles for their consumers. Toyota is the first automobile manufacturer in the global market to develop and produce a supplemental restraint system rear-seat center airbag. The purpose of the airbag is to reduce the severity of rear-seat passenger injuries in a side-on collision, such as when one passenger strikes another. This is a revolutionary initiative within the automobile industry.

Toyota's Strength, Weaknesses, Opportunities and Threats

"This is one of those horrifying nightmare problems that will occasionally occur, no matter how hard you try," said David Cole, chairman of the Center for Automotive Research; alluding to Toyota's massive recalls coupled with quality and component failures. Automotive analysts recognize the technological capability and innovativeness of Toyota but couldn't comprehend why the organization should allow defective components to slip through their production lines. Some experts call Toyota's massive quality failure as unacceptable and unpardonable. While some experts are critical about Toyota, others are reasoning with the organization by pointing to the fact that the components in Toyota automobiles didn't fail in isolation, they failed because other components played a critical role in the failure. "It's not that they didn't design a good accelerator pedal or linkage or floor mat or heater," said Steven D. Eppinger, professor of Management Science and Engineering Systems at Massachusetts Institute of Technology (MIT). "They designed them each quite well. But the most difficult problems always relate to interactions between components and other systems." Toyota engineers were blamed for their accelerated testing which makes it impossible to test every component in a timely manner. The good thing for Toyota was the fact that the organization was able to publicly admit the quality failure which didn't tarnish much of its reputation.

Toyota will remain the most competitive automobile manufacturer in the global market place for decades to come because of its strong financial condition as well as its aggressive innovation strategies that are designed to help solve environmental problems around the world. Toyota will remain the most viable automobile manufacturer because of its quest for continued employee training and development. According to Peter Senge, the best companies are those that always make developing internal talents a high priority. Toyota has all the characteristics of a learning organization and this puts the organization in a different level in the world of innovation. One of the biggest strengths within Toyota is that innovation appears to be a culture and tradition.

China and other emerging markets in Asia and Central South America promise to become a strong engine for the future growth of Toyota. This is a potential big market for the organization. Toyota appears to have all the business opportunities in the global market place because of its strategic business model designed toward product oriented management. The organization is placing greater emphasis on market needs based on the customer first philosophy. Most business analysts predict a high future demand for hybrid and compact vehicles for the organization because of the increase awareness of environmental friendly products and services in the global market place.

The only foreseen threat for Toyota is the fact that other automobile manufacturers are entering the hybrid market. The market may become saturated and may draw down prices and services. Right now, Toyota is dominating the hybrid automobile market.

Summary

The unparalleled global economic crisis significantly impacted Toyota's profitability in fiscal year 2009 resulting in massive operating losses in the company's history. In spite of the massive operating losses in fiscal year 2009, the organization is re-focusing for a quick recovery in sales and earnings by accurately responding to the structural shifts in demand with profit improvement initiatives. Toyota has established emergency profit improvement committees to ensure the massive operating losses in fiscal year 2009 do not re-occur. To further address fiscal year 2009 operating losses, Toyota has established three fundamental financial management strategies that will allow the organization to achieve steady and sustainable growth and more importantly to increase corporate value. The three key financial management strategies include growth, efficiency and stability.

With the aggressive growth strategy, the organization seeks to provide high quality, affordable, and attractive automobiles that meet customer's needs in each country and region and to further the early commercialization of next-generation technologies in the areas of environment, energy, and safety. With the efficiency strategy, Toyota seeks to improve profitability and capital efficiency. Improving capital efficiency entails the maximization of unemployed and idle facilities in all its global operations. In addition, the efficiency strategy calls for an aggressive cost cutting initiatives in business processes that do not add value to the organization.

This chapter explored what Toyota is doing different in leading the hybrid automobile industry. I have also examined what innovation means to Toyota's executives. I have thoroughly examined why Toyota is considered a learning organization and how the organization has built quality into its business processes. Innovation ecosystem has been explored within Toyota; what innovation ecosystem means to the organization. Finally, I have re-evaluated the organization's strengths, weaknesses, opportunities and threats as the global leader in hybrid automobile manufacturing technologies.

End Notes

1. Toyota President, Akio Toyoda: 2009 Annual Report pp3.
2. Toyota 2009 Annual Report pp23.
3. International Organization of Motor Vehicle Manufacturers (2010). Automotive Issues in the World. Retrieved October 26, 2010 from: http://oica.net
4. Sousa, M.C. (2006). The sustainable innovation engine. The Journal of Information and Knowledge Management Systems, 34(6), pp398.
5. Toyota 2009 Annual Report.
6. Toyota Corporate Profile (2010). Why Hybrid? Retrieved October 27, 2010 from: www.toyota.co.jp
7. Senge, P.M (1997). Creating learning communities. Executive Excellence, 14(3), 17-18.
8. Senge, P.M (1997). Creating learning communities. Executive Excellence, 14(3), p17.
9. Liker, J.K., & Meier, D. (2007). *Developing your people the Toyota way.* McGraw-Hill: Black lick, OH.
10. Senge, P.M (1997). Creating learning communities. Executive Excellence, 14(3), p17.

11. DeGraff, J., & Quinn, S.E. (2006). Leading innovation: How to jump start your organization's growth engine. McGraw-Hill: Black lick, OH.
12. DeGraff, J., & Quinn, S.E. (2006). Leading innovation: How to jump start your organization's growth engine. McGraw-Hill: Black lick, OH.
13. Senge, P.M (1997). Creating learning communities. Executive Excellence, 14(3), p17.
14. Toyota Chairman Fujio Cho remark in 2009 Annual Report pp1.
15. Senge, P.M (1997). Creating learning communities. Executive Excellence, 14(3), p18.
16. Desouza, K.C., Dombrowski, C., Awazu, Y., Balor, P., Papagari, S., Jha, S., & Kim, J.Y (2009). Crafting organizational innovation processes. Innovation Management Policy and Practice, 11(1), 6-33.
17. May, M.E. (2006). The elegant solution: Toyota's formula for mastering innovation. Free Press: New York.
18. National Research Council (US). Committee on Comparative Innovation Policy, Best Practices for the 21st Century. Report of a 2007 Symposium.
19. Toyota 2009 Annual Report: pp: 34.
20. Toyota 2009 Annual Report.
21. Senge, P.M. (1997). Creating learning communities. *Executive Excellence, 14(3), 17-18.*
22. Rose, R.C., Kumar, N., & Pak, O.G. (2009). The effect of organizational learning on organizational commitment, job satisfaction and work performance. *The Journal of Applied Business Research, 25(6), 55-65.*
23. Kaur, M., & Narang, S. (2009). Shareholder value creation in India's most valuable companies: An empirical study. IUP Journal of Management Review, 8(8), 16-42.
24. Lombard, R. (2002). Creating shareholder value. Accountancy Ireland, 34(3), 8-10.
25. Bear, S., Rahman, N., & Post, C. (2010). The impact of board diversity and gender composition on corporate social responsibility and firm reputation. Journal of Business Ethics, 97(2), 207-221.
26. Boddy, C.R., Ladyshewsky, R.K., & Galvin, P. (2010). The influence of corporate psychopaths on corporate social responsibility and organizational commitment to employees. Journal of Business Ethics, 97(1), 1-19.

4 – Why Microsoft is Considered Number Four Most Innovative Company

C ontinuously meeting the needs of customers are key for gaining and keeping customers in today's workplace. "Continuous innovation is the engine that drives highly successful companies such as Apple, General Electric, Google, Honda, Hewlett-Packard, Microsoft, Procter & Gamble, Sony, Tata group and many others. Innovation is an especially potent competitive weapon in tough economic times because it allows companies to redefine the marketplace in their favor and achieve much needed growth. However, achieving continuous innovation is very hard, and most attempts fail. One increasingly popular way to think about innovation is to conceive of it as an open rather than a closed system. To continue to be innovative in a world of widely distributed knowledge, many companies are recognizing that they must open their innovation process to combine internal with external R&D. That can be done by bringing in new human capital, engaging in strategic alliances or acquiring technology ventures. By the same token, internal inventions that a company decides not to pursue should not simply be shelved, but rather considered for commercialization through licenses, spin-offs or joint ventures. If an open innovation system does in fact help drive growth and performance, managers need to answer two critical questions: 1. which innovation strategies should the company pursue? 2. Which innovation strategies go well together?" [1]

Chapter Learning Objectives

- Being aware of how Microsoft is oiling its innovative engine as an innovation champion.
- Exploring Microsoft's revenue generating business segments.
- Understanding Microsoft's strategies as a learning organization where employee training and development are fundamental.
- Gaining an elementary comprehension of how Microsoft is leading the innovative cloud computing transformation.
- Understanding the increasing importance of how Microsoft is delivering new advances across innovative product portfolio.
- Recognizing Microsoft's record financial performance in spite of the global financial Tsunami.
- Explaining Microsoft's strategy as champion of innovation.
- Understanding how Microsoft is innovating to improve the planet.
- Examining Microsoft's strengths, weaknesses, opportunities, and threats in the global market place.

Introduction

Innovation is the primary source of U.S. economic leadership and the foundation for organizations competitiveness in the global marketplace. Organizations' investment in research and development and the Government's strong intellectual property laws and efficient capital markets are among the reasons that America has for decades been the best at transforming new ideas into successful businesses. The most important factor in every innovative initiative is the workforce. Every innovation strategy is built upon a talented and diligent workforce within the organization. The global economy benefits as more people acquire the skills needed to foster innovation. If organizations are to remain competitive, they will certainly need a workforce that consists of the world's brightest minds[2]. Innovation is the foundation for Microsoft's success. Microsoft's model for growth is fundamentally based on the organization's ability to initiate and embrace disruptive technological trends, to penetrate into new markets; both in terms of geographies and product areas. Microsoft maintains a long term commitment to research and development across a wide spectrum of technologies, tools, and platforms spanning from communication and collaboration, information access and organization, entertainment, business and electronic commerce, advertising as well as devices.

Another reason Microsoft is successful in computing innovative technologies is that the organization adopts a global approach to innovation. Even though the organization's main research and development facilities are located in the United States, Microsoft operates research facilities in other parts of the U.S and around the world. This global approach to innovation helps the organization sustain its competitive advantage in local markets as well as enables the organization to continue to attract talented workforce across the global markets. The organization invests in innovation by focusing on emerging technological trends and breakthroughs that they believe offer the greatest opportunity to deliver value to their end users as well as foster the growth of the organization. Microsoft research is one of the world's largest computer science research organizations. These research organizations work in close collaboration with top universities around the world to advance the state-of-the-art in computer science by providing a unique perspective on future technology trends[3].

"The question of which innovation strategies to pursue is critical, because corporate executives have multiple strategies for achieving innovation at their disposal. They can decide to spend more on internal R&D, hire and retain the best human capital, ally with innovative companies or buy innovation through acquisitions"[4]. Based on strategic assessment of key technology trends and broad focus of long term research, development and innovation of new products and services, Microsoft has seen a significant opportunity in the following fields of computing: 1) cloud computing and software plus services, 2) natural user interfaces, 3) new scenario innovation, and 4) intelligent computing.

Microsoft Case Study – What Microsoft is doing to Stay Innovative and Unravel Competition?

Microsoft is the world's largest software, service and solutions company headquartered in Seattle Washington. Microsoft was founded in 1975 with the mission of enabling people and businesses throughout the world realize their full potential. As of June 2009, the organization has a full time worldwide workforce of 93,000. The composition of the workforce is 56,000 in the United States and 37,000 in other global locations. Further breakdown of the workforce include 36,000 in product research and development, 26,000 in sales and marketing, 17,000 in product support and consulting services, 5,000 in manufacturing and distribution and 9,000 in general and administration. One of the organization's successes is its ability to attract and retain talented and qualified workforce. In addition to attracting and retaining talented workforce as a competitive advantage, none of the organization's 93,000 employees are subject to collective bargaining agreements.

Technological innovation is the organization's foundation for long term growth and survival. Because Microsoft's innovativeness has proven to sustain its competitive advantage, the organization intends to maintain its commitment to investment in research and development, engineering excellence, as well as the delivering of high quality products and services to customers and partners. One of the organization's primary business objectives is to help accelerate worldwide personal computer adoption and software upgrades. Microsoft continues to advance the functionality, security, and value of Windows operating systems and more importantly has remained focused on selling products and services in emerging markets in order to reduce the amount of unlicensed software used in those markets. "We also continue to develop innovative software applications and solutions that we believe enhance information worker productivity, improve communication and collaboration in work groups, aid business intelligence, and streamline processes for small and mid-sized businesses."[5] To sustain its competitive advantage in the face of aggressive competition from other competitors of proprietary and open source software, Microsoft's primary objective is to deliver products and services that provide the best platform for network computing thus software that is easier to deploy and manage, and more importantly make software available to global markets that is secure with the lowest total cost of ownership.

Microsoft is aggressively investing in research and development to further enhance its existing and new lines of products and services including cloud computing, search online solutions, business solutions, mobile computing, communication, entertainment and other business areas that the organization believes may sustain its long term competitiveness in the global market place. In addition, creating opportunities for its partners and delivering products and services that exceed customers' needs is the organization's priority. The organization works diligently to provide superior quality products and services to its customers and to create opportunities for its partners through its integrated platform.

How Microsoft Is Oiling Its Innovation Engine?

Why does Microsoft innovate? According to Koudal and Coleman (2005), Microsoft innovates because the organization is seeking the right to market. Koudal and Coleman (2005) label Microsoft as an innovation champion because innovation champions are special organizations with distinct structure and characteristics. In order to be labeled a champion organization in this competitive global market place, organizations must have an outstanding procedural and resource support as well as social and cognitive support[6]. Microsoft maintains its innovation championship because of its amazing social contacts, depicted through the number of communities and global markets in which the organization does business. Microsoft innovation success depends primarily on its innovation centers around the world. According to Microsoft Corporate Vice President "as knowledge and innovation become the primary catalysts for economic growth, the Microsoft innovation centers can play a vital role in generating powerful new ideas through training, education and knowledge transfers." You cannot generate good innovative ideas if you don't have the right people with the right skill set and expertise to ask the right questions and design appropriate solutions for them.

Microsoft oils its innovation engine by utilizing ideas from students, entrepreneurs, academics, professional software developers, startup businesses, information technology professionals, industry organizations as well as local governments. The local innovation centers around the world promote skills and intellectual capital among industry partners. For example, in Brazil alone, more than 14,000 students and information technology professionals have collaborated with the organization on new technologies and through this collaboration, the students and professionals have received advanced training in new technologies and business skills which are designed to help Microsoft innovate new products and services.

Microsoft innovation centers are not only designed to oil the organization's competitiveness, they are designed to contribute to the economic development and prosperity of local economies around the world. For example, in Malaysia several students and individuals have participated in a four month internship at Microsoft innovation centers where they've learned how to work with powerful software development tools and were mentored by experienced information technology professionals. From the experience these individuals have gained, they were able to start their own software companies that contribute to the local software economy in Malaysia's[7]. According to the Director of Microsoft European Innovation Center, "in leading the European Microsoft Innovation Center forward, our focus will be on driving collaboration with other Microsoft Research labs to advance technologies and make them accessible to a broad population." The Director adds that they will leverage the advancement of technologies by building on the existing organization's research assets, by validating their efforts within customers' environments; and ultimately transferring their development work to Microsoft product groups.

Microsoft innovation lab in Cairo has been instrumental in tapping potential talents from the Middle East and Africa. The lab's focus is on applied research and development initiatives aimed at building a strong local talent for Microsoft's concept driven innovation. Another way by which Microsoft oils its innovation engine is through its procurement process. The revolution of enterprise innovation is not new to Microsoft. Microsoft has been the pioneer of enterprise innovation. Microsoft has revolutionalized enterprise innovation by standardizing its procurement practices. In addition, the organization has empowered its workforce to act as agents on behind of the organization. For example, certain employees are authorized to approve transactions with vendors without seeking management approval. This enables Microsoft's development and engineering processes to continue uninterrupted.

Microsoft Innovative Operating Segments

The organization has five dependent innovative operating segments namely Client, Server and Tools, Online Services Business, Business Division and Entertainment and Devices Division. Each of these segments provides senior management with a detailed financial projection of their business operations. Most of the innovative work is carried out and implemented in all or one of the segments. For example, the client segment has the responsibility for all the technical architecture, engineering, and delivery of the organization's Windows product; while the server and tools segment develops and markets software server products.

1. Client Segment. The client segment within the organization is responsible for the technical, engineering, and delivery of the organization's Windows product family and is also responsible for the organization's relationship with personal computer manufacturers, including multinational and regional equipment manufacturers. Microsoft reports that in fiscal year 2009, majority of the organization's revenues came from the sales of Windows Vista, which was released in 2007. The client business segment faces tremendous competition from companies such as Apple, Canonical, and Red Hat. In spite of the tremendous competition, Microsoft's operating system products compete effectively by offering innovative software, giving customers choice and flexibility, easy to use interface, compatibility with a broad range of hardware applications, as well as the largest support network for any operating system.

2. Server and Tools. The sever and tools segment develops and markets software server products, software developer tools, services, and solutions. The organization provides a wide range of consulting services and offers product support services that help customers in developing, deploying, and managing the organization's server and desktop solutions. In addition, Microsoft offers training and certification to developers and information technology professionals about their server and tools. Half of Microsoft's server and tools revenue comes from multi-year licensing agreements; 20 percent is purchased via fully packaged product and transactional volume licensing programs. Some key organizational servers and tools include Windows Server Operating System, Microsoft SQL Server, Visual Studio, Silverlight and many others. Microsoft server operating system products and services face a tremendous competition from wide range of operating system servers and applications provided by companies with a variety of marketing

and promotional strategies. Competition from vertically integrated computer manufacturers such as Hewlett-Packard, IBM, as well as Sun Microsystems offer their own versions of UNIX operating system pre-installed on server hardware. Almost all of the competition provides some sort of server hardware for the Linux operating system and a quite number of the competition contribute significant amount of expertise and input in the development of the Linux operating system.

3. <u>Online Services Business</u>. Microsoft online services business is made up of an online advertising platform with offerings for publishers and advertisers. The organization's information offering services and search engine such as Bing was designed to take some market share away from Google. Microsoft refers to Bing as a "decision engine" meaning it helps information seekers and researchers to organize and present information in a relevant and meaningful manner. Bing home page appears to be more spectacular than other popular search engines. It shows videos, landscape, shopping, entertainment and what have you. Other information offering services such as MSN Portals and channels, personal communication services such as email and instant messaging are designed to help keep people contacted around the world. Others include, Microsoft AdCenter/adExpert, Microsoft Media Network, Mobile Service, MSN Hotmail Plus and what have you. Microsoft earns revenue primarily from online advertising, including search, display, and email and messaging services. The organization also earns revenues from this segment through subscriptions and transactions generated from online paid services, such as advertiser and publisher tools, digital marketing and advertising agencies.

Microsoft increases its client base through behavioral targeting. In order to reach wide client base, the organization has recently updated the behavioral targeting tools and has also launched new releases of MSN properties worldwide. Microsoft aggressive competitors in this online services business segment include AOL, Google, Yahoo! And other websites and portals that offer content as well as online services of all types to clients. Microsoft competes with all these organizations to provide advertising opportunities to clients. Microsoft believes strongly that it can compete aggressively with these organizations. Some of the organization's aggressive competitive strategies are to provide software innovation in the form of information and communication services that will assist end users find and use the information and experiences they acquire online and more importantly provide end users with effective advertising results via improved systems and after sales support.

4. <u>Microsoft Business Division</u>. This innovative business segment is made up of Microsoft Office System and Microsoft Dynamics Business Solutions. The products and services under this segment are designed to increase individual, team, and organizational productivity via a wide range of programs, services as well as software solutions. This innovative business segment generates more than 90 percent of the organization's revenues. The ability of Microsoft to generate over 90 percent of revenues from this segment is primarily due to the organization's ability and capability of adding value to the core office product set and more importantly, the ability of aggressive expansion of product offerings in professional areas such as content management, enterprise search, collaboration, unified communications as well as business intelligence[8.] The organization's products and services such as Microsoft Dynamics products provide end users with innovative business solutions for financial management, customer relationship management, and supply chain management, analytics applications for small and mid-size businesses as well as large organizations and divisions of global enterprises. Some key products and services under this business segment include the innovative and award winning Microsoft Office; Microsoft Office Project; Microsoft Office Visio; Microsoft Office SharePoint Server, FAST ESP; Microsoft Exchange Server; Microsoft Exchange Hosted Services and many others. Competitors in this business segment include companies such as Adobe, Apple, Corel, Google, IBM, Novell, Oracle, Red Hat, Zoho, as well as local applications developers in Asia and Europe[9]. Microsoft vows to continue to invest aggressively to

uniquely respond and exceed market demands for additional functionality, products and services. The organization will continue to compete aggressively with notably vendors in segments such as content management, enterprise search, collaboration tools, unified communications as well as business intelligence. Some notably competitors in business intelligence segment include Cisco, SAP, IBM, Oracle and Endeca. Microsoft has been successful in competing with these organizations because of Microsoft's strategy of providing flexible easy to use solutions that operate well with technologies platforms that end users have already implemented in their organizations.

5. Entertainment and Devices Division. The primary role of the entertainment and devices division within Microsoft is to develop, produce, and market the Xbox video game system including consoles and accessories; third party games, games published under the organization's brand; Xbox live operations, research sales and support for those products and accessories. In addition to developing, producing, and marketing the aforementioned products and services, this business segment is responsible for offering PC software games, online games, media room, internet protocol television software, surface computing platform, mobile and embedded device platforms and many others. This segment is one of the most competitive business segments within the organization. Price competition is the wide spread competition among organizations in this business segment. Microsoft competes aggressively in this segment by providing wide variety of innovative products and services, accurate timing of product releases as well as effective and marketing and distribution strategies. Microsoft faces substantial competition from the following organizations in this segment: Apple, Google, Nokia, Openware Systems, Palm, Qualcomm, Research In Motion and Symbian. Microsoft competitive advantage in this business segment depends primarily on the organizations ability to provide exclusive game content that gamers are seeking, in addition, Microsoft's ability to provide unique computational power as well as console reliability is significant. Microsoft competitive advantage in this

business also emanates from the organization's ability to provide significant innovation in hardware architecture as well as the provision of exclusive content from the organization's own game franchises[10].

Microsoft as a Learning Organization

Microsoft is considered a learning organization because it understands business cycles and risk management. "Consistent investment in risk management training and systems, and the creation of a risk culture that everyone in the organization understands and takes responsibility for are critical for future successes.[10]". Every employee within Microsoft is responsibility for the future success of the organization. Employees are empowered, trained and re-educated in fundamental risk management strategies to ensure that risks are mitigated. They are also trained to ensure that risks that arise in one particular business segment are completely controlled so that they don't re-emerge in other functional areas or segments. Investing in future leaders of the organization is Microsoft's business. Genuine learning organizations such as Microsoft, sees learning and employee development opportunities in all segments of the organization. Management works diligently to ensure that every employee takes full advantage of the learning opportunities available in order to improve their respective business segments. In the global market place, organizations do not learn in isolation, they learn alongside with their employees and senior executives. While training employees is absolutely crucial to executing the day-to-day mission of Microsoft, preparing employees and the organization for the future means, taking employee training needs to the next leve[11].

According to Cordivari (2010), a learning organization is more future focused and combines basic and ongoing training and employee development and engagement initiatives into a systematic results oriented approach that begins even before an employee is hired. The challenge Cordivari (2010) adds is to create and nurture a culture that reinforces the idea that there are no limits to what can be accomplished within Microsoft if employees take full advantage of available opportunities through management motivation and empowerment. Microsoft understands that organizational learning improves business operations, sustains competiveness and eliminates inefficiencies.

Leading the Innovative Cloud Transformation

According to CEO Steven A. Ballmer, Microsoft has seen long contraction and expansion throughout the history of the computing industry. Key breakthroughs in the history of Microsoft include the microprocessor in the 1970s, the graphical user interface in the 1980s, and the Internet in the 1990s. These breakthroughs have revolutionized the role that information technology plays in how Microsoft manages information, run the various business segments, share experiences and what have you. These key breakthroughs have brought a dramatic positive change in the lives of millions of people worldwide. Microsoft is in the wave of yet another innovative and great transformation in the field of cloud computing.

"The cloud is revolutionizing computing by linking the computing devices people have at hand to the processing and storage capacity of massive datacenters, transforming computing from a constrained resource into a nearly limitless platform for connecting people to the information they need, no matter where they are or what they are doing. This has profound implications for the way people use technology across their lives to work, learn, communicate, and have fun.[12]" With Microsoft's outstanding financial and human resources capability, the organization seeks to grow and shape this revolutionary innovation of cloud computing rather than ride with it. According to Mr. Ballmer, this is the reason why the organization has made a company-wide commitment to Microsoft's solutions, bringing the benefits of the cloud to the billion people who use computing today and the billions more who will gain access to digital technology for the first time in the years ahead. In fiscal year 2010, Microsoft invested $8.7 billion in research and development, with most of that devoted to cloud technologies.[13] The approximately 70 percent of Microsoft's 40,000 engineers work on cloud-related products and services, and in fiscal year 2011 that number is expected to grow to nearly 90 percent according to Mr. Ballmer.

Microsoft started investing in cloud computing approximately 15 years ago. In the global market environment, Microsoft's cloud technologies and services support hundreds of millions of customers. More than 300 million people use Windows Live® Hotmail and Windows Live Messenger to send nearly 10 billion messages every day[14]. This year, Microsoft's Xbox LIVE® subscription base surpassed 25 million subscribers, a growth of over 20 percent from last year.

Currently, over 10,000 corporate customers have adopted Windows Azure and thousands of businesses and government departments and entities representing millions of people have acquired Microsoft's online productivity services to improve productivity and reduce costs. Customers include 13 of the top 20 global telecom firms, 15 of the top 20 global banks and 16 of the top 20 global pharmaceutical companies. Together, these technologies, products, and services enable Microsoft to do something no other company can do thus, deliver cloud solutions that span the complete range of business needs the organization customers anticipate. Microsoft strongly believes the impact of cloud computing will be as big or bigger than the previous waves of technological change. The opportunities cloud computing will create for the organization customers, partners as well as the entire organization will be immense. When it comes to the cloud, "we're all in" says Mr. Ballmer.

Delivering New Advances across Innovative Product Portfolio

Microsoft has seen the strongest growth in the history of the organization in fiscal year 2010 in spite of the global financial crisis. Windows® 7 tops the list of the innovative products and services for the fiscal year. Faster, simpler, and easier to use; Windows enables people to work the way they want to and more easily than ever before. Windows® 7 has already sold 175 million copies, making it the fastest-selling operating system in history[15]. Fiscal year 2010 also saw updates of many of the organization's Windows Live cloud services, which are redefining how people socialize, communicate and share experiences.

Late in fiscal 2010, Microsoft released Office 2010 with Office Web Apps. This newest version of the organization's world-leading productivity software provides a unified experience that enables people to connect to their work and each other across the PC, phone and browser so they can get things done from almost anywhere. Even before its official launch date, Office 2010 had been downloaded by more than 9 million beta customers.[16] Along with the several releases of products and services, in fiscal year 2010 Microsoft laid the groundwork for several products that will continue to deliver innovation over the next several years. Microsoft has rolled out

Kinect™ for Xbox 360®, a new experience that incorporates video and audio sensors to empower people to use gestures and voice commands to play games and enjoy other kinds of TV entertainment – all without the need for a controller.

Record Financial Performance

The enthusiasm, focus and strong commitment from every employee within Microsoft have enabled the organization to achieve record financial results for the fiscal year 2010 in spite of the financially troubled global economy. For fiscal year 2010 revenues reached a record $62.5 billion, an increase of 7 percent compared with the previous fiscal year. Operating income grew by 18 percent to $24.1 billion. Diluted earnings per share jumped 30 percent to $2.10 and the organization returned almost $16 billion to shareholders through stock buybacks and dividends.[17]

These outstanding results reflect the strong product momentum, innovation and creativity across the entire organization. Microsoft achieved double-digit growth in every business segment during the fourth quarter of fiscal year 2010 in spite of the financially troubled global economy. In addition, Microsoft grew operating income more quickly than overall revenue during each quarter of fiscal year 2010; which demonstrates that Microsoft has maintained a tight focus on cost reduction as well as quality of service.

For over 35 years, Microsoft helped launch the first great wave of information technology transformation by creating the software that made the PC revolution possible. With the help of the committed client based as well as the organization's outstanding customer service coupled with the industry-leading cloud solutions, exciting product portfolio and strong financial performance, Microsoft is playing a key role in delivering the tools and technologies that are making information technology more powerful, more useful, more affordable and more accessible.[18]

Microsoft as a Champion of Innovation

According to Howell (2005), 90 percent of raw ides never go beyond the idea generator's desk. Only three percent of the remaining 10 percent obtain sufficient backing to become projects with less than 1 percent being commercially launched. Howell (2005) argues that one reason for the high failure rate of new ideas is their failure to attract a champion.[19] Dedicated champions are pivotal to innovation success and thus must be supported in their efforts and integrated into the mainstream of organizational operations.[20] Microsoft's investment and design of the innovative cloud computing, Windows 7, the incomparable decision engine known as Bing, the development of business intelligence products and services and the design and development of a host of other outstanding products and services indicate that Microsoft is a champion of innovation. Championing innovation must become a norm in organizations and not an episodic event that relies on happenstance and a strong minded individual expending large amounts of effort. Innovation champions are active in supporting innovation and seeking out opportunities, but they need to be encouraged and motivated by management.[21] Innovation is a tradition and a norm within Microsoft. In fiscal year 2010 alone, Microsoft invested $8.7billion in research and development; this is to ensure that the right ideas get to commercialization quicker.

How Microsoft is Innovating to Improve the Planet

Microsoft is committed to the innovation of software and technologies that will help end users and businesses in the global market improve and safe the planet. The primary goal for the organization is reduce the negative impact of their operations and products and pioneer responsible environmental leadership. Microsoft has implemented numerous programs to reduce its environmental footprint. The following are the major initiatives designed to reduce the negative impact of the organization's products on the environment:

1. Microsoft Generation 4.0 Datacenter Vision. This is one of the sustainable initiatives Microsoft has embarked to make its datacenters more environmental friendly. The vision is for all datacenters within the organization be made more efficient in order to reduce the energy needed to operate those datacenter.

2. Saving Energy and Carbon in the Cloud. Cloud computing is the innovative way of responding to the negative impact of datacenters on the environment. The operation of datacenters is well known to be environmentally unfriendly. With cloud computing, end users and businesses do not need hardware or software. Cloud computing has no physical location unlike

datacenters. Processing of data is carried out in the "cloud." Cloud computing technology utilizes utility computing model meaning end users are charged based on utilization. Microsoft has commissioned a lifecycle analysis (a study that calculates the environmental impacts of a product or service across its entire lifecycle), conducted by Accenture and other organizations. The results of the study indicate that cloud computing has the potential to reduce a company's energy use and carbon emissions. For example businesses choosing to run Microsoft's Business Productivity Online Services, such as Exchange Online and SharePoint Online, or Microsoft Dynamics CRM Online can reduce energy use and their carbon emissions by at least 30% per user compared to an average on-premise installation of those applications (datacenters). Organizations that utilize cloud computing will realize benefits in energy efficiency, reduce energy costs, and will play a significant role in the sustainability of information technology.

3. Recycling Programs and Substance Policies for Hardware Products. Microsoft supports the proper recycling, recovery, and handling of waste associated with electronics. Microsoft implements strict policies to ensure that their products and packaging fully comply with the requirements of each government's jurisdiction in which the organization does business. Microsoft restricts substances and other materials from its products as required by law and in certain instances, exceeds regulatory requirements. In addition Microsoft's mandatory recycling obligations, the organization offers information as well as funds programs to help end users and businesses voluntarily recycle their Microsoft branded hardware and other products.

4. Microsoft Carbon Footprint Disclosure. Microsoft has implemented a policy of voluntarily measuring its carbon footprint and provides annual reports on its greenhouse gas emissions to the Carbon Disclosure Project (CDP). The Carbon Disclosure Project is an independent non-profit organization holding the largest database of primary corporate climate change information in the world. The organization is headquartered in London with offices around the world.

Thousands of businesses and corporations in the global market measure and disclose their greenhouse gas emission and climate change strategies through CDP.

5. <u>Microsoft Smart and Sustainable Building Practices</u>. Microsoft facilities and campuses adhere to policy guidelines aimed at reducing environmental footprint. This means the organization's facilities are green building compliant.

Microsoft's Strength, Weaknesses, Opportunities and Threats

Microsoft financial and human resource capability is unmatched. This is a unique strength and opportunity for the organization. With the global population reaching nearly 6 billion, serves as tremendous market opportunity for this innovation champion. Microsoft ability to turn innovative products and services quickly to commercialization is one of the biggest strengths that the organization can boast of. The organization's presence in almost every global market and more importantly the worldwide acceptance of the technology in every global market is strength for this innovation champion. In the competitive global market today, the use of information technology is a requirement in determining organizational success. No organization today operates without information technology and or without business intelligence technologies. This is where Microsoft emerges. Microsoft's strengths and opportunities cannot be overemphasized in the global market place. Customer loyalty is an unmatched strength that industry competition cannot fight away from Microsoft. The organization has diligently built over time a strong loyal customer base that may take competition some enormous amount of resources and time to take away from this innovation champion. The organization's outstanding marketing and distribution system is unbeatable. Strong global demand for the organization's products and services is unstoppable.

In spite of the aforementioned strengths and opportunities for Microsoft, the organization is not without weaknesses and threats. The first threat is the introduction of low cost, low quality technology products and services in the Asian and European markets. Another threat is the persistent lawsuits and class action suits by group of individuals and industry competitors in order to distract management focus. Violation of intellectual property rights in the global market place is another significant threat for the organization. This may include piracy as well as other unlawful use of the organization's products and services. Many competitors have labeled Microsoft as a monopoly but have failed to investigate the origin of that accusation. The marketing and distribution strategy of Microsoft has been described by many as overly aggressive without respect for end users and competition. Microsoft has been described as an organization that tries to do everything and anything related to technology thereby overstretching employees. Microsoft has been described as an organization that bundles most its products and offers no alternatives for their end users.

Microsoft is significantly exposed to economic risk from foreign currency exchange rates, interest rates, credit risk, equity prices, and commodity prices risks. Even though Microsoft discloses that a greater portion of these risks have been hedged, however, they may still impact results of operations such as cash flows and financial conditions.

Summary

Innovation is essential to retain and improve organizations market and competitive positions, and as such requires maximum internal support so that the current poor translation rate from idea to product is reduced.[21] The tremendous reduction of idea to product rate is what makes Microsoft the most innovative company in the software industry coupled with the huge capital outlaw that is being poured into research and development annually. Microsoft has proven time and time again that research and development and human resource development are what are keeping the organization competitive in the software development industry. The billions of dollars in revenues that the organization recognizes annually come from these five innovative business segments: client segment, server and tools segment, online services business segment, Microsoft business division as well as the entertainment and devices division. Each of these innovative business segments provides management with comprehensive financial view of key businesses in all the functional areas. The segments also enable the alignment of strategies and objectives across the functional areas.

Microsoft's fundamental mission is to enable people and businesses throughout the world to realize their full potential in information technology and business intelligence. Microsoft's success is dependent primarily on delivering breakthrough innovation and high quality value solutions through its integrated software platforms. In this chapter, I have examined in great depth how Microsoft is oiling its innovation engine as an innovation champion; I have explored how and why Microsoft is considered a learning organization. In this section, I reviewed the historical and present breakthroughs within the organization. Microsoft's ability to deliver new advances across innovative product portfolio; examined fiscal year 2010 strong financial performance in spite of the financially troubled global economy. I have also explored Microsoft's innovative cloud computing technologies as well as the initiatives designed to improve the planet. Finally, I looked at the organization's strengths, weaknesses, opportunities and threats in the global market place.

Endnotes

1. Rothaermel, F.T., & Hess, A.M. (2010). Innovation strategies combined. MIT Sloan Management Review, 51(3), 12-15.
2. Gates, B. (2007). How to Keep America Competitive. Retrieved November 28, 2010 from: www.washingtonpost.com
3. Microsoft Corporation 2009 Annual Report.
4. Rothaermel, F.T., & Hess, A.M. (2010). Innovation strategies combined. MIT Sloan Management Review, 51(3), pp14.
5. Microsoft Corporation 2009 Annual Report – pg1.
6. Koudal, P., & Coleman, G.C. (2005). Coordinating operations to enhance innovation in the global corporation. Strategy and Leadership, 33(4), 20-32.
7. Microsoft Corporate Profile. www.microsoft.com
8. Microsoft Corporation 2009 Annual Report.
9. Microsoft Corporation 2009 Annual Report.
10. Githens, B. (2010). RMA is a learning organization. The RMA Journal, 92(7), 8-8.
11. Cordivari, R. (2010). From training company to learning organization. T+D, 64(1), 60-60.
12. Microsoft Corporation 2010 Annual Report
13. Microsoft Corporation 2010 Annual Report
14. Microsoft Corporation 2010 Annual Report
15. Microsoft Corporation 2010 Annual Report
16. Microsoft Corporation 2010 Annual Report
17. Microsoft Corporation 2010 Annual Report
18. Microsoft Corporation 2010 Annual Report
19. Howell, J.M. (2005). The right stuff: Identifying and developing effective champions of innovation. Academy of Management Executive, 19(2), 108-119.

20. Coakes, E., & Smith P. (2007). Developing communities of innovation by identifying innovation champions. The Learning Organization: The International Journal of Knowledge and Organizational Learning Management, 14(1), 74-85.
21. Coakes, E., & Smith P. (2007). Developing communities of innovation by identifying innovation champions. The Learning Organization: The International Journal of Knowledge and Organizational Learning Management, 14(1), 74-85.

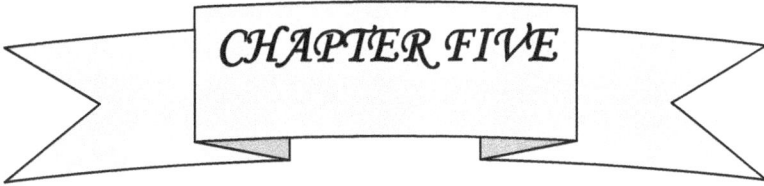

CHAPTER FIVE

5 – Why Nintendo is Considered the Fifth Most Innovative Global Company

M anaging product innovation stems from effective management and organizational culture. Innovation is the lifeblood of organizations in the global market place; being at least one step ahead of competitors is the route to survival and longevity. There's nothing new about the realization that product innovation is key to building businesses, creating employment opportunities as well as building national economies. There is no surprise in the fact that people can, given the right resources, motivation, empowerment, and conditions, come up with amazing inventions which can change people's lives for generations to come and more importantly, generate tremendous revenues for the organizations in the fortunate position of innovating, designing and delivering those products onto the market before anyone else has time to come up with something similar. Evidence shows that businesses that have the awareness to continually create, evaluate and successfully exploit their new ideas are more likely to survive and prosper in today's ever changing global marketplace.[1]

Chapter Learning Objectives

- Comprehending the amazing journey of Nintendo into the world's most innovative manufacturer of interactive home entertainment and its competition.
- Exploring how Nintendo is leading the motion sensing technology through its interactive home entertainment console.

- Examining how Nintendo is oiling its innovation engine in the global market place.
- Understanding the single most important study that explores the rate of social acceptance of video games in homes.
- Recognizing Nintendo as a learning organization as well as the elements that make a learning organization.
- Gaining elementary comprehension as well as defining the dimensions of organizational learning and innovation within Nintendo.
- Exploring the environmental footprint and safety of Nintendo products.
- Recognizing Nintendo's Strength, Weaknesses, Opportunities and Threats in the interactive home entertainment industry.

Introduction

Being an entrepreneur has to do with seeing what others have not seen, trying to make something out of nothing, projecting into the future, getting into the minds of people and making the best out of every situation. Entrepreneurship also includes the spirit of creativity, innovativeness and pursuit of excellence. These are vivid description of the founder of the fifth most innovative multinational organization in the global market place. Everyone would have been successful if success was easy. Success begins with a dream, pursuing the dream with passion and courage. In pursuing the dream along the way an individual is faced with challenges and opportunities. The initial dream might turn into multiple smaller dreams as exemplified in Nintendo's pursuit of excellence and success in the interactive home entertainment industry. The mission and philosophy of Nintendo America is to produce and market the best product and support service available to consumers. The organization believes that it is essential not only to provide products of the highest quality, but to treat every customer with attention, consideration and respect. Constantly listening to customers helps improves organization's products and services. The organization feels an equal commitment to its talented and diligent employees around the world. It's interesting to witness innovation and creativity in Nintendo. How an organization that almost went out of business had learned from its mistakes and re-organized itself to become the world's most innovative and competitive organization in the interactive entertainment industry.

Nintendo Case Study – What Nintendo is doing to Stay Innovative and Unravel Competition?

Nintendo is a multinational organization and a worldwide leader in the creation and manufacturer of interactive entertainment. The organization also manufactures and markets hardware and software for its popular home video game systems. As a wholly owned subsidiary, Nintendo of America, based in Redmond, Washington, serves as the headquarters for Nintendo's operations in North America. The organization's worldwide operation is headquartered in Kyoto Japan. According to Boston Consulting Group, Nintendo is the fifth most innovative organization in the global marketplace. Founded in 1889 by an energetic and visionary entrepreneur called Fusajiro Yamauchi; as of 2010, the organization had 4,130 employees worldwide with total operating income of $6.5 billion and total assets of $19.8 billion.[2] Mr. Yamauchi had tried several business ventures just to live up his dream during the 19th Century. The name Nintendo according to senior executives means "Leave Luck to Heaven" which further explains the difficulty and challenges of being an entrepreneur. The organization has several diverse portfolios including stakes in Major League Baseball and others.

Nintendo started its operations earlier as a card company in the 19th Century; it designed manufactured and marketed handmade playing cards in Japan. As time went on the organization experienced tremendous demand in handmade playing cards. Nintendo hired more employees to help meet the increasing demand of their high quality handmade playing cards in Japan and in the world. The organization's success during its formation was primarily based on the quality of its inputs. It was reported that the founder didn't have heir to take over the operation of the business. Because he didn't have an heir, he adopted his son-in-law who took over the operation of the business when he retired in 1929. With the organization's tremendous success in handmade playing cards, it started to diversify into other business operations such as TV network, marketing instant noodles and management of Cab Company. The diversification was a failure because of the business model that was put in place. With the vision and passion for success, Nintendo management didn't give up; Nintendo got into the manufacture and distribution of toys with the help of its skilled engineers. Nintendo engineers during the 60s invented several popular toys with mechanical extending arm. The manufacture and distribution of the mechanical extending arm was a success which gave the organization the confidence as well as the needed resources to get into the gaming industry. Nintendo got into the gaming industry by establishing coined driven video games with the younger generation as their target market. Targeting the younger generation with the coined driven video game was a successful business model.

In the 20th Century, the grandson of the founder Hiroshi Yamauchi traveled to North America to explore and learn more about the playing card industry. When he visited North America he learned process control and cost effectiveness and how an organization can do more with little resources. In addition to learning how to operate cost effectively; his visit opened several opportunities including gaining access to the main characters of the world's largest family entertainment and media enterprise – World Disney. The inclusion of Disney's main characters in the organization's playing cards drove sales through the roof for the organization. After the organization's successful business model of targeting younger generation with its coined driven video games, Nintendo game popularity in the global market by nearly monopolizing the interactive entertainment industry with the production of the following innovative products and services:

The innovative Nintendo Entertainment System was introduced in 1985. When it was introduced in 1985, it revolutionized the video game industry. It sold over 60 million units and people brought games like Mario and Zelda into their homes for the first time. The introduction of the innovative Game Boy in 1989 was a huge success for the organization. The design and manufacture of Game Boy device defined portable gaming in the home interactive gaming industry. It sold over 150 million devices worldwide, originally bundled with the game Tetris. The release of Super Nintendo Entertainment System gave gamers more gaming capability because of the 16-bit technology. The organization sold 49 million units of Super Nintendo Entertainment System worldwide because of the game's flexibility. 1996 witnessed the release of the innovative Nintendo 64. N64 established new standards in realistic 3D gaming. Several products were released between 1996 and 2006 including the Game Boy Pocket, the Game Boy Advance, and Nintendo Game Cube. In 2006 Nintendo launched the Wii. Wii is a home game console designed to compete strongly with Xbox 360 (Microsoft) and PlayStation 3 (Sony). Wii broke several sales records in the global market place because its revolutionary features. Innovative features such as Wireless motion-sensitive remote controllers, built-in Wi-Fi capability, as well as other innovative features have made the Wii the best-selling generation console system in the world.

Nintendo innovation team is getting creative every day working diligently to produce design and technology that no video game company has ever produced. Nintendo has revolutionalized home video game by making it an ageless game unlike a decade ago where video games were only played by kids. According to market researchers, the global video game industry is estimated to be bigger than the entire Hollywood. Video game technology and innovation have gone beyond entertainment. Video games have proven to help train the U.S Army and also help in the rehabilitation of wounded soldiers. Nintendo has designed its video games to play either on a computer or on a console. Consoles are devices designed to display signals which are used to view video games. Not many companies make the video game console. Apart from Nintendo, the other organizations that make video game consoles include Microsoft and Sony.

Pioneers of Motion Sensing Technology

Nintendo and its innovation team are working tirelessly to capture or monitor the heartbeat of gamers in order to determine the level of excitement or relaxation that Nintendo Wii provides. Monitoring gamers' heartbeat while they play could lead to future medical breakthrough in gamers' health. The motion-sensitive control technology is what Nintendo innovation team is looking to advance probably into advance medicine in the future and more importantly to broaden the video game market. In an interview, Nintendo CEO was asked whether the organization has any future plans to make the organization's products High Definition. The CEO's response:

If we have an opportunity to make a new console, it will probably support HD because it is now common throughout the world. However, as far as the Wii is concerned, we have not found a significant reason to make it HD-compatible at this time. What is the significant meaning to the users? I don't think we should do it unless we find that reason. If we decide for other reasons to make new hardware, then HD is one of the things we would naturally add[3].

In a similar interview, the CEO was asked what the organization is doing to stay competitive in the ever changing global market and not rest on its laurels. The CEO responded:

If we stay in the red ocean, then free games would have an impact on our business. There are countermeasures to this. If we fail to provide experiences that can never be duplicated by free games, then we will not be able to survive. I don't think that free games are something new. On the PC, there have always been free games. But finding them was not always easy. With the popular products like the iPhone, now it is easier. Apple has highly promoted the size of its free software library, so people are becoming aware of it. My opinion is that the iPhone has suddenly changed the picture. We are asking people to pay. Getting people to pay is always a matter of survival. We have to provide something new and surprising. We cannot stay where we are today. We have to be different tomorrow[4].

How Nintendo Is Oiling Its Innovation Engine?

Forward thinking and continuous innovation is the key survival tool for organizations in the 21st Century. Nintendo, with its long history in business understands that the only way it can survive is to embrace innovation as part of doing business. "Corporations must train and develop employees on how to look beyond the "now' and be future thinkers" (Ricardo 2010, p.17)[5]. Nintendo's tremendous success in the interactive video game industry is based on the effective implementation of the following concepts:

1. <u>Creativity, Innovation and Entrepreneurship</u>: Nintendo is fully aware of the needs and wants of its target market. When an organization understands the needs and wants of its customers, the next thing to do is to create an environment that empowers employees to design and develop new products and services. Empowering and training employees within an organization increases self-esteem and more importantly promotes teamwork and commitment to the organization. Nintendo has internally developed entrepreneurs and innovators to visualize the global market for new products and services. This team of innovators and entrepreneurs within Nintendo consistently goes into the minds of customers and projects what products and services they might need five and ten years down the road; and with the organization's strong financial positions empowers the teams to design and produce those products and services before someone else does that. Failure of multinational organizations to create breakthrough inventions can be understood through either their lack of motivation – economic perspective or lack of ability – organizational perspective.[6] Nintendo's success emanates from its pool of internal ability as well as its open leadership of employee empowerment. According to Sakar, Echambadi & Harris (2001), pro-activeness is one facet of the multidimensional concept of entrepreneurship along with autonomy, innovativeness, risk-taking propensity, and competitive aggressiveness[7]. For example, a highly proactive organization may not be as innovative or aggressive, yet it may be considered entrepreneurial in terms of its initiatives. Nintendo success is primarily based on its ability to act as an aggressive and innovative organization.

2. <u>Employee Development</u>: Nintendo's success and amazing innovation in the home video game industry is much attributed to the level of its human resource management. "Human capital is the most expensive resource any corporation can possess. People are the backbone of any company, whether designing, producing, or selling; it is people who do the work. The marketing and accounting departments must track trends and organize environments for increased business" (Ricardo 2010, p.13). The research and development team must get into the

minds of consumers to project what they might need five years, ten years or fifteen years down the road. This needs skilled, talented and motivated workforce to carry out this responsibility. Nintendo ensures that its workforce no matter the level of responsibility is well motivated, empowered and trained to make certain decisions without having to go through several approvals. The role of employee development within Nintendo cannot be overemphasized – persistent innovation through its skilled workforce is what gives Nintendo the marked edge over its competition. It's an inherent desire of most employers to continue the learning and skill development process of their employees. Inability to provide this opportunity can give rise to employee dissatisfaction, deterioration of morale as well as excessive turnover[8].

3. Ethical Standards of Behavior: Many of the ethical issues in international business are rooted in the variations among nations in their political system, law, economic development, and culture. What is considered normal practice in one nation may be considered unethical in another[9]. Nintendo management realizes the importance of doing business in a sound ethical environment. Nintendo leadership also recognizes the variation in international ethical standards. The violation of several international ethical standards may lead one to question that there is no international ethical standards. Do organizations exist to violate employees' rights knowingly? Or do they exist to exploit employees? Do organizations exist to deceive consumers? Do organizations exist to knowingly pollute the environment without considering the consequences of their violation? Studies indicate that most organizations are fully aware of their ethical violations. When they engage in unethical behaviors, they do know that they are engaged in unethical business conduct. Hill (2009) reported in mid-2006 systematic labor abuses at the factory in China that made the iconic iPod for Apple computers. According to the reports, workers at Hongfugjin Precision Industries were paid as little as $50 a month to work 15-hour shifts making the iPod. In addition, there were reports of forced overtime and poor living conditions.

As noted earlier, for employees to be innovative and creative they must work in conducive work environments; they must be empowered, trained and motivated. Several studies confirm that a happy worker is a creative and innovative worker. Nintendo ensures that its contractors and subcontractors are carefully screened to ensure that employees are compensated based on their skill level and experience. They are provided with good working conditions and more importantly, they are well trained to promote the mission of the organization. Nintendo leadership takes ethical violations seriously. Lack of ethical standards within an organization hinders innovation and creativity. Unethical corporate behavior is often associated with unrealistic expectations that if the company cuts costs and corners it will provide stakeholders with greater profits. This can certainly be the case in the short term, but in the long run such behaviors could prove disastrous for the company[9]. The costs of such behaviors in the long run outweigh the benefits. Retards innovation and creativity, may lead to serious liability payment, drop in stock prices if a public company and what have you.

4. Teamwork: Teamwork is one of the major concepts that Nintendo uses to oil its innovation engine. "Teamwork is generally associated with groups of people gathered together to work on a project, meet an objective, or be part of a department or division. Rarely do you find an organization or business that does not rely on collective efforts of employees to solve problems" (Ricardo 2010, p.14). Newly hired engineers in Nintendo receive on the job training by working collaboratively with small teams that include experienced engineers who serve as mentors. Working collaboratively across functional areas within Nintendo is what makes the organization nimble and creative. Skills and expertise are pulled together across functional areas to resolve an issue. Ideas are shared in teams and groups. Encouraging teambuilding among employees and understanding each other's strengths and weaknesses is what sets Nintendo aside from its competition in terms of innovation and creativity. Nintendo culture is different from most multinational organizations; there is no silly or stupid idea within the organization. Leadership takes every idea seriously

until it's proven otherwise especially at the brainstorming stages where an issue is at stake. Therefore, for an organization to oil its innovation engine, employees must be encouraged to work in teams and groups, freely share ideas among each other and must ensure that no idea is considered silly or unwise.

5. Effective Communication: No creative or innovative idea can be developed without making it known to those who need to know. The importance of communication in innovation process cannot be overemphasized; understanding the importance of formal and informal communication in the workplace is critical to the successful implementation of every innovation program. Nintendo management understands that effective communication across functional areas is one of its strengths in implementing its aggressive innovation programs. Ricardo (2010) reports that communication is the way innovative organizations share information. Organizations that are most innovative and productive create a climate for sharing ideas. Innovative organizations understand that formal and informal ways of communication are important in developing a means where ideas and policies move freely to those who need the information. Every functional area within Nintendo shares information across the board. For example, the accounting and finance departments share revenue trends; they also share financial projection trends as well as the financial position of the organization. The engineering departments share their research and development initiatives to those that need the information. Identifying and sharing key information with those who need the information is important.

Social Acceptance of Video Games/Entertainment

It's obvious that Nintendo leads the console industry however; the organization recognizes that more work and research still need to be done to increase the social acceptance of video games in homes. In 2009, Nintendo conducted telephone and mail survey to evaluate social acceptance of video games in the United States. The results were not very encouraging. Nintendo sampled 4,656 participants and found that 18 percent of Americans said they liked video games very much while 33 percent said they liked movies very much. The results for music lovers were very encouraging. In all, almost 50 percent of Americans said they loved music very much. The 2009 survey had set new product development levels for the organization. In an interview immediately after the survey results were released the CEO acknowledges that "of course, we should try our best to produce appealing products which keep users excited, but on the other hand, it is a big problem if such excitement causes family troubles or affects a user's life balance," The CEO added "I believe that the social acceptance of video games will never improve if we just aim for user absorption without being aware of the potential problems." With the astonishing results of the survey, Nintendo considered implementing a game timer (similar to that of the Xbox 360's "Family Timer") to allow parents to limit the time that kids could spend playing. However this idea was scrapped because of how players would feel if the game suddenly stopped during an exciting part according to the CEO. Alternatively, a time log was implemented that could let parents review the amount of time that was spent playing games. Similar options are currently being explored for the 3DS.

With 18 percent of acceptance rate, Nintendo realizes the challenge ahead and has mounted an aggressive campaign to expand the demography of consumers enjoying video games. The organization is encouraging people around the world regardless of age, gender, language, cultural background or gaming experience to embrace and enjoy video game as a mode of family entertainment. Even though with the 18 percent acceptance rate, the organization believes a lot has been achieved in bringing video games to homes around the world. Nintendo and its innovation team are working diligently to further the penetration of Wii by encouraging communication in the living room of each household through continuous software launches that will tremendously amaze gamers with brand new game play. As part of the campaign to increase acceptance of video games in homes, the organization has released Nintendo 3DS that allows gamers to play video games in 3-D without the need for any special glasses. Nintendo believes that the release of 3DS will offer gamers an innovative game play.

Nintendo as a Learning Organization

The re-organization of Nintendo into a pioneer organization in the video game industry indicates that Nintendo is obviously a learning organization. The introduction of Wii into the global market which has successfully competed with Sony and Microsoft indicates that continuous learning, technology and aggressive innovation are part of the tremendous success that Nintendo is achieving in the current global market place. No organization will achieve this level of success in the global market place without being a learning organization. Learning organizations have gained popularity in today's competitive global environment. Being called a learning organization is one, practicing the principles and concepts of learning organization is another. Learning organizations must enhance their learning capability and must be able to learn better and faster from their successes and failures both within and outside their organizations (Rijal, 2010)[10]. Many management scholars and researchers affirm that organizational culture, strategy, structure and environment in which an organization functions more often than not influence the development and implementation of a learning organization.

From handmade playing card company to the world most innovative organization in the interactive home entertainment industry shows Nintendo's capability as well as management amazing strategy in learning from their successes and failures both within and outside their organization. Learning from failures and successes cannot be implemented organization-wide without good leadership and vision. Nintendo management has demonstrated good leadership in executing strategies to stay competitive and profitable. For two consecutive years – 2007 and 2008, Nintendo was honored with Emmy Award for excellence in engineering creativity and innovation for the release of Nintendo Wii (Corporate Profile) [11]. Technological and Engineering Emmy Awards are organized annually to recognize multinational and domestic organizations for excellence in technological innovation and creativity. According to the vice president of U.S Operations "the pioneering interfaces for Wii and Nintendo DS reflect our long tradition of seeking new ways to enhance the gaming experience for users at every level".

Dimension of Organizational Learning and Innovation in Nintendo

Dimension of organizational learning and innovation are the basic concepts that lay the foundation for creativity, learning and innovation. Organizational learning occurs when an organization develops and applies new knowledge that has the possibility of changing employees' behavior; which results in strengthening and repositioning the organization to achieve improved results; nimbleness to change by creating results oriented employees who see change as an opportunity to sustain the competitive advantage of their organization. An organization learns when its employees are continuously creating, organizing, storing, retrieving, interpreting and applying information. This information becomes knowledge (and hopefully wisdom) about improving the working environment, improving performance, improving business processes, and achieving long-range goals that will make the organization achieve its strategic mission and vision in the marketplace (Shahin & Zeinali, 2010). Nintendo understands that sustain its competitiveness depends on the caliber of workforce that it has within the organization. The following are the main dimensions of organizational learning and innovation within Nintendo:

1. *Strategy*: This dimension was important for Nintendo's because the organization used this dimension to disrupt the interactive entertainment industry by aggressively learning through consumer surveys to target non-gamers with its Wii console. The processing power of Wii and its award winning interactive features overshadowed Microsoft Xbox and Sony's PlayStation. Nintendo also uses this dimension to make its prices more competitive. Nintendo understands that price and quality are important in making purchasing decision. Nintendo product prices are competitive as compared to its competition.

2. *Structure*: This dimension spells out the ultimate decision making process within the organization. Nintendo management is structured in such a way that no single individual can significantly influence the organization at the executive level as compared to other multinational organizations where a single individual has overwhelming authority at the executive level. All decisions are made jointly at Nintendo; this is because of the pass failures of organizations where all final decisions had to come from one individual.

3. *Support Mechanism*: Nintendo has a well established support mechanism to help achieve its vision. Understanding end-user needs and designing appropriate measures to resolve them are important for the survival of an organization especially in the

highly competitive industry such as the interactive entertainment industry. Nintendo management realizes that it needs effective and functioning support mechanism to help sustain its competitive advantage. Because of that Nintendo has developed support mechanisms such as technology support, customer support, management training, sales support, marketing and financial support to help make its products and services available to end-users with high quality and competitive pricing.

4. *Behavior*: Employee behavior within an organization determines the dimension of learning and creativity. Employee behavior is a vast construct that touches almost all parts of human resource management in today's tech savvy workforce. In almost every organization, employee behavior is built on the foundation of earlier concepts like job satisfaction, employee commitment and Organizational Citizenship Behavior, innovation and creativity. Most management studies indicate that employee behavior is a stronger predictor of positive organizational performance clearly showing the two-way relationship between employer and employee (Markos & Sridevi, 2010)[12]. A satisfied worker is a well behaved worker because they don't want to violate policies and procedures; they respect management and authority because management has earned the respect and commitment from those workers. Markos & Sridevi (2010) maintain that engaged employees are emotionally attached to their organizations and are highly involved in their job with a great enthusiasm for the success of their employer, going extra mile beyond the employment contractual agreement. Nintendo employees have almost always gone the extra mile to understand the mission and vision of the organization; where the organization wants to be in five and ten years is the concern of employees as well as management because management constantly communicate the vision and mission to them. Employees within Nintendo are motivated, well trained and empowered to do their job. Nintendo has a great employee retention programs designed to retain talented and skilled employees. This program starts the very day new

employees are hired, designed to build positive relationship between the employee and their respective management.

5. *Teamwork*: Teamwork is one of the dimensions of organizational learning and innovation within Nintendo. Most occupational psychologists emphasize the importance and benefits of teamwork for every member on the team as compared to Taylorized or Taylorism division of labor concept where each and every member concentrates only on one aspect of the task. Nintendo management always ensures that teamwork is properly managed to yield higher job satisfaction, creativity, and innovation. The variety of team projects and tasks assigned within Nintendo are designed to encourage individual team members to learn and use different skill sets and more importantly team members are constantly rotated between projects to minimize the boredom and stress of repetitive work. There are job enrichment programs across every functional area in Nintendo in order to increase satisfaction and learning.

6. *Innovating Leadership*: This is a critical dimension within Nintendo because innovation leaders are identified and trained right from the first day of employment. Innovation and organizational learning is a top down management strategy in order to ensure everyone within the organization to given the opportunity to share their inherent talents and skills to sustain the competitive advantage of the organization. Innovation and organizational learning is ineffective without management support. This is why innovation and organizational learning is one of the major traditions within Nintendo.

7. *Continuous Learning*: Continuous learning as part of the dimension of organizational learning and innovation occurs when organizations seek to stay competitive and innovative in their respective industries due to the ever changing needs of consumers and competition. According to London & Smither (1999) in continuous learning organizations such as Nintendo, there is an organization-wide concept, value, belief, and expectation that general knowledge acquisition and application is important in achieving organizational mission and vision[13]. To ensure successful implantation of continuous learning

concept within Nintendo, management always provides the needed resources in the form of financial resources or budgets to help explore hidden talents in each individual within the organization. Because of the annual budget for continuous learning within Nintendo, management encourages every employee to make continuous learning part of their job responsibilities which is supported by managers and supervisors.

8. *Product Development*: Organizations that create products and services without an active involvement of the customer may not get the product to commercialization; this is due to consumer sophistication and changing needs and wants. In developing a product, Nintendo ensures that it learns and adequately understands the needs of the end-user. Nintendo's tremendous success in the home video game industry depends largely on the organization's ability of co-creating its products with end-users in every stage of the product development.

9. *Product Marketing*: The purpose of product marketing as a dimension of organizational learning and innovation within Nintendo is to create exchanges that satisfy consumers and organizational objectives. Nintendo achieves product marketing in two ways: 1) through communication and 2) through operation. The communication aspect primarily involves information via price, promotion, product labeling and packaging. The information is passed to the end-user is designed to position the product in the market and to persuade present and potential end-users to patronize the product and or service. Nintendo has a unique way of persuading end-users especially the potential ones to trial their product and or service. Differential utility is the innovative approach Nintendo uses to lure potential customers to their products and services. With differential utility technique, Nintendo compares and contrasts its products and services with the competition. This technique provides a clear distinction between Nintendo's products and services with those of the competition.

10. *Sound Decision Process*: According to Hill (2004), making decisions that work and are implemented are a key organizational competency within Nintendo. The interesting

aspect of sound decision making in Nintendo is that more often the decision that need to be made requires technical knowledge however; the decision sometimes needs to be implemented by those with less technical knowledge which appears to be common in most organizations. No decision is made within Nintendo without the involvement of the key people. Nintendo ensures that when a decision is made, it's a sound representation of all those involved.

Nintendo and the Environment

Many multinational organizations are nervous in making assertions about their product safety to consumers and the environment. Nintendo is one of the few multinational organizations that have publicly declared the environmental footprint of their products as clearly stated below:

> We would like to assure customers that we take our environmental responsibilities seriously and are rigorous in our commitment to comply with all relevant laws relating to environmental and product safety, including avoiding the use of dangerous substances in our manufacturing processes and ensuring the safe disposal and recycling of materials. We consider the environmental impact of our products over their entire life cycle, from planning to disposal. In the planning phase, for example, we make every effort to design energy-efficient products and select materials for component parts and packaging materials with careful consideration for the environment. We also consider the importance of reducing environmental impact at end-of-life disposal by clearly indicating the materials used in each product to make recycling easier. We also work to eliminate harmful substances from our products right from the initial stages of material selection and have established strict environmental control standards, with our 340 production partners all co-operating with us in our efforts.

Nintendo's Strength, Weaknesses, Opportunities and Threats

Strengths

Strong balance sheet and cash flows for research and development

Highly motivated, skilled and empowered workforce

Democratic leadership

Strong product demand

Diverse workforce

High quality products and competitive pricing

Very collaborative organization

Promotes the concept of teamwork

Effective program for workforce training and development

Outstanding product differentiation – motion sensing

Quick commercialization of innovative products

Weaknesses

Unable to meet product demand

Dependence on outside manufacturers

Lack of software variety

Opportunities

Huge untapped market segments

Few competition

Difficulty for new entrance

Ability to maximize profits

Exploring new demography of gamers - Adults and older people

Threats

Changes in accounting standards and taxation systems. Conflict of views between Nintendo and global tax authorities may cause additional tax costs

Leakage of personal and confidential customer and employee information

Product liability

Limitation of enforcing intellectual property rights

New entrants and global market fluctuation

Foreign exchange fluctuation

Summary

Nintendo has demonstrated to the global market place and competitors that it's an organization of continuous learning where employee development and customer satisfaction are priority. Nintendo tremendous success in the global market place is attributed to its passion for excellence, innovation and creativity. From handmade playing card company to the world most innovative organization in the interactive home entertainment industry shows Nintendo's capability as well as management amazing strategy in learning from their successes and failures both within and outside their organization. Learning from failures and successes cannot be implemented organization-wide without good leadership and vision. Nintendo has demonstrated that continuous learning and aggressive innovation are the solution to longevity and profitability in the interactive home entertainment industry.

In this chapter I examined the amazing journey of Nintendo into the world's most innovative manufacturer of interactive home entertainment and its competition. I explored how Nintendo is leading the motion sensing technology through its interactive home entertainment console, reviewed how Nintendo is oiling its innovation engine in the global market place as well as sharing the single most important study that explores the rate of social acceptance of video games in homes around the world.

This chapter has also covered the elements of learning organizations and why Nintendo is considered a learning organization. We have gained elementary comprehension as well as examined the definition of the dimensions of organizational learning and innovation within Nintendo. The last part of the chapter explored the environmental footprint and safety of Nintendo products as well as addressed Nintendo's Strength, Weaknesses, Opportunities and Threats in the interactive home entertainment industry.

End-Notes

1. Bradford (2008). Survival through innovation. Microsoft and Nintendo strive to offer the latest "must haves." Strategic Decision, 24(1), 21-24.

2. Nintendo Corporate Profile: Retrieved December 1, 2010 from: http://www.nintendo.com/

3. Takahashi, D. (2009). Nintendo CEO: Wii care about your heartbeat, but not your iPhone, the recession or free games. Retrieved December 28, 2010 from: www.venturebeat.com

4. Anantula, S. (2006). Lessons of innovation from Nintendo Wii. Retrieved December 28, 2010 from: www.worldisgreen.com

5. Ricardo, H.P. (2010). Developing a comparative edge through employee value: How all international companies should conduct business. The Business Review, Cambridge, 16(1), 11-17.

6. Ahuja, G., Lampert, C.M. (2001). Entrepreneurship in the large corporation: A longitudinal study of how established firms create breakthrough inventions. Strategic Management Journal, 22(6/7), 521-543.

7. Sakar, M.B., Echambadi, R., & Harrison, J.S. (2001). Alliance entrepreneurship and firm market performance. Strategic Management Journal, 22(6/7), 701-711.

8. Hill, C. (2009). Global business today. New York: McGraw-Hill/Irwin.

9. Ricardo, H.P. (2010). Developing a comparative edge through employee value: How all international companies should conduct business. The Business Review, Cambridge, 16(1), 11-17.

10. Rijal, S. (2010). Leadership style & organizational culture in learning organizations: A comparative study. International Journal of Management & Information Systems, 14(5), 119-127.

11. Nintendo Corporate Profile. Retrieved December 21, 2010 from www.nintendo.com

12. Markos, S., & Sridevi, M.S. (2010). Employee engagement: The key to improving performance. International Journal of Business and Management, 5(12), 89-96.

13. London, M., & Smither, J.W. (1999). Empowered self-development and continuous learning. Human Resource Management, 38(1), 3-15.

Appendix

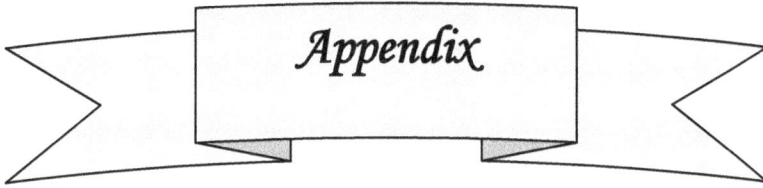

Author Biography

Osman Gunu is an Accountant and Financial Policy Analyst for the United States Department of Agriculture – Forest Service. Osman is responsible for the agency-wide development and issuance of financial management policy and accounting standards. He interprets cash management regulations and guidelines from the U.S Code, U.S Treasury, Office of Management and Budget (OMB) and from the Code of Federal Regulation (CFR) as well as from other federal authoritative bodies.

Osman is a doctoral candidate in Business Administration with a focus on Management. He received his Master's and Bachelor's degrees from George Mason University in Fairfax, Virginia. Osman's dissertation findings were accepted for presentation at the International Academy of Business and Public Administration Discipline (IABPAD) 2011 conference in Dallas, Texas. He has published several financial policy handbooks and manuals for his agency and is an active member of National Society of Collegiate Scholars.

Index

Innovation does not always require an instruction manual. Innovation requires a mindset for *effectiveness* (doing the right things), *efficiency* (doing things right), as well as the ability to proactively *anticipate* customers' needs and wants, and *convert* this knowledge into useful products and services in a timely manner.

(Bahaudin G. Mujtaba, Professor of Management)

www.ingramcontent.com/pod-product-compliance
Lightning Source LLC
Chambersburg PA
CBHW031946190326
41519CB00007B/677